T0339095

WRITERS ON WRITERS

Roy Foster *On Seamus Heaney*

John Burnside *On Henry Miller*

Michael Wood *On Empson*

Colm Tóibín *On Elizabeth Bishop*

Alexander McCall Smith *What W. H. Auden Can Do for You*

Michael Dirda *On Conan Doyle*

C. K. Williams *On Whitman*

Philip Lopate *Notes on Sontag*

EVA HOFFMAN ◈ **ON CZESŁAW MIŁOSZ**

Visions from the Other Europe

PRINCETON UNIVERSITY PRESS

Princeton and Oxford

Published by Princeton University Press
41 William Street, Princeton, New Jersey 08540
99 Banbury Road, Oxford OX2 6JX

press.princeton.edu

Library of Congress Cataloging-in-Publication Data

Names: Hoffman, Eva, 1945– author.
Title: On Czesław Miłosz : visions from the other Europe /
    Eva Hoffman.
Description: Princeton : Princeton University Press, [2023] |
    Series: Writers on writers | Includes bibliographical references.
Identifiers: LCCN 2023005046 (print) | LCCN 2023005047 (ebook) |
    ISBN 9780691212692 (hardback) | ISBN 9780691230412 (ebook)
Subjects: LCSH: Miłosz, Czesław—Criticism and interpretation. |
    Polish literature—20th century—History and criticism.
Classification: LCC PG7158.M5532 H64 2023 (print) | LCC PG7158.M5532
    (ebook) | DDC 891.8/5173 [B]–dc23/eng/20230331
LC record available at https://lccn.loc.gov/2023005046
LC ebook record available at https://lccn.loc.gov/2023005047

British Library Cataloging-in-Publication Data is available

Editorial: Ben Tate and Josh Drake
Production Editorial: Kathleen Cioffi
Text and Jacket Design: Wanda España
Production: Danielle Amatucci
Publicity: Alyssa Sanford and Carmen Jimenez
Copyeditor: Daniel Simon

This book has been composed in Minion Pro Regular

Printed on acid-free paper. ∞

Printed in the United States of America

10 9 8 7 6 5 4 3 2 1

⊞ ON CZESŁAW MIŁOSZ

First, there was the person. I met Czesław Miłosz in 1981, shortly after he emerged from near-total obscurity to win the Nobel Prize in Literature at the end of 1980. I was sent to interview him in his Berkeley home by the *New York Times*; eventually, a profile based on the meeting came out in the newspaper's Sunday magazine. The setting was spectacular and incongruous: high up in the Berkeley hills, at the top of a steep road called Grizzly Peak Boulevard, and looking out on the ocean from one side. Both the beauty and the incongruity—of Berkeley, of California, of America itself—were explored repeatedly in his poems and essays. I prepared myself carefully not to act as intimidated as I felt, but there was really no need. There was something about Miłosz that refused homage. Maybe it was his directness, and his frank, youthful vitality. Or perhaps the total lack of pretension with which he talked about himself. He was not overwhelmed by the Nobel—nor did he underplay its importance. No false modesty, no excessive pride: just a man among men, a person whose task, to which he tirelessly devoted himself, was writing.

I think both the vitality and a sense of measure—moral, intellectual, aesthetic—were the sources and drivers of much of his writing; even, paradoxical as it may seem, his most complex forms of expression and thought. His body of work is huge, both in its scope and variety of genres: he wrote essays, novels, political reflections, autobiography, and, above all, poetry. He translated quantities of poetry from other languages. When I expressed my amazement at the size of his output during that two-day conversation in his Berkeley home, he told me that writing was his work, and he approached it as a worker would his job. He wrote for a certain number of hours (in the morning, as I remember) each day. There was no pretension to anything more romantic, or anguished, or a claim to inspiration. Miłosz disliked pretension of all kinds, and he valued work—honest work, he might have said, work that involved "shaping matter"—greatly; it is one of the themes recurring throughout his writing. Indeed, it is an interesting aspect of his oeuvre that despite its formal variety and inventiveness, there was great consistency of themes and concerns in all the genres he explored, including the most exceptional, and for him the primary form of poetry. He was not interested in formal experiment for its own sake: he wanted meaning, and he wanted truth; and he derived both, in whatever form, from the ground up, from himself and his own experience, from direct observation and the pressure, the logic, of thought. But then, his experience was vast and his erudition enormous.

When I met Miłosz, he was at a late stage of a long, winding, cross-continental, history-spanning trajectory. A trajectory that in all its aspects—personal, political, intellectual and poetic—was crucially affected by his origins in Lithuania and Poland; that is, in "the Other Europe." It was also a biographical narrative that, in its geographical progression and some of its thematic concerns, had surprising similarities to my own and that, for me, made his work—particularly in its exilic phases—both a literary and personal illumination. That this should be so is itself of more than personal interest. Across the catastrophic chasm of World War II, Poland remained part of "the Other Europe"—a condition crucial to Miłosz's perspective that, even in my postwar generation, continued to be a formative fact and a difference that mattered.

I cannot hope, in this short book, to encompass all of Miłosz's writing, nor would I have the presumption to try. But I will follow, through his poetry and prose, what for me is Ariadne's thread of a parallel trajectory, hoping it will lead to some insights about this most complex of twentieth-century poets and men.

▦ "I am here." Thus, the opening sentence of a collection of essays titled *Visions from San Francisco Bay*. A sentence that could not be simpler, but which for Miłosz—as perhaps for many other exiles—would have held dimensions of meaning. A kind of fundamental amazement: How is it that I am here, rather than anywhere else? And what *is* here, what is this bay at which I'm looking, this Berkeley, this California—this America? The rest of this slim but densely perceptive book is an exploration of these questions, in their geographic, cultural, and personal meanings. "The human imagination is spatial," Miłosz writes in a chapter entitled "Where I Am"; and the significance of place and the conceptual structures shaping our imagination of inner and cosmic space are some of the governing themes within his enormous body of work. Exile—the process of being uprooted from one's original culture, language, political systems, and, crucially for Miłosz, landscapes— sharpens such forms of awareness. It undermines the sense of absoluteness of any one place or country, a process that is often personally painful but can be very useful for a writer. Being dis-placed gives you a perspective and a point of view. It was perhaps for the advantages of defamiliarization that writers such as Joyce and Beckett chose exile. Miłosz didn't choose it, nor did he court detachment, never mind Romantic or modernist alienation, but his multiple transplantations broadened and deepened his vision beyond most of his contemporaries. "We are not suited to the long perspectives," wrote Phillip Larkin, that quintessentially English poet. But Miłosz came by his telescopic vision naturally, or rather, through the force of circumstance.

Long before exile, there was the place of origin: the Place, to which Miłosz comes back again and again, in poetry and prose, in imagination and memory. "Between the ages of seven and ten I lived in perfect happiness on the farm of my grandparents in Lithuania," Miłosz writes in a late essay titled "Happiness." "It was long ago, and huge oaks and lindens made my fairyland, while orchards allowed me to discover the taste of apples and pears of many species. . . . I lived without yesterday or tomorrow, in the eternal present. This is, precisely, the definition of happiness. . . . It was, I do not hesitate to say, an experience of enchantment with earth as Paradise. . . . A path in the shade of oaks led down to the river, and my river was never to abandon me throughout my life, wherever fate carried me, even during my years on the far shores of the Pacific."

Rivers—or perhaps versions of that original river—run throughout Miłosz's poetry with their ceaseless, Heraclitean flow: "Under various names, I have praised only you, Rivers! / You are milk and honey and love and death and dance," he writes in a poem called "Rivers" (1980). In "Happiness," he asks himself if he is mythologizing; he hopes not. He was opposed to all sentimentality and excess, including that of nostalgia. But while exile makes for an almost inevitable detachment from the place of arrival, it often reinforces the primacy, or a kind of absoluteness, of the place one was forced to abandon—the original Place. When you grow up close to the streets and landscapes where you were born, you can observe how they change, sometimes gradually, sometimes more suddenly. You can accept the facts of change—or you can sometimes long for an Elsewhere. But in exile, stored only in memory, one's original childhood paradise (if you're lucky enough to have grown up happily) remains unchanged, Edenic. As for rivers— especially those original ones—they seem to hold a special place in the human imagination.

Some, like the Jordan and the Ganges, are considered holy, and many of the earliest cities were built near them for their life-giving power. When I was writing about my own emigration, it was the memory of my childhood rivers that stood for sheer aliveness and pleasure. And it was perhaps not accidental that when I wrote about the discomfiting distance from the second language which all emigrants initially experience, the sense of separation between word and reality was exemplified in the word "river"—which, in English, for a long time failed to evoke an actual river as the Polish word *rzeka* did.

Exile relativizes everything, except, perhaps, the intensity of early memories. It is in his clearly autobiographical novel, *The Issa Valley*, under the guise of a protagonist who is ostensibly not himself, that Miłosz allows himself an almost Nabokovian lyricism of memory. And in his descriptions, he also reveals himself to be a highly knowledgeable naturalist. "In the meadows, the faint whir of snipe, the gabble of blackcock, so like a bubbling on the horizon, and the croaking of frogs (the number of which has something to do with the storks that nest on the rooftops of cottages and barns) are the voices of that season when a sudden thaw gives way to the blossoming of cowslips and daphne—tiny pink and lilac blossoms on bushes as yet without leaves." So he writes in the opening pages of *The Issa Valley*, and he goes on to describe a region of superstitions and belief in magic, a place where Christianity still clashed with earlier, pagan beliefs. In other words, an earlier place, not yet touched by industrialization or modern technologies. Miłosz certainly didn't share in the superstitions, but there were qualities of that earlier world, and particularly of peasant life, that he valued—and defended. Attachment to a specific place; closeness to nature; working on a human scale and in a known, familiar community; and above all, working with the land and producing something from it. "Until recently," he writes, "everything a man needed was manufactured at home."

An earlier place: even across the great chasm of World War II, the villages of my childhood remained so. That virginal, fast-running river, the thickly wooded forest, riding in hay-filled carts, barefoot kids and peasants singing their wild atonal tunes as they returned from their work in the evening—these are all part of my psychic endowment, and it is clear to me why Miłosz returned to his early memory sites again and again. Is it only for a child that such places hold their enchantment? Or for the visitor from the city, longing to "get back to nature"? For the inhabitants of those villages, their charm couldn't rival the appeal of modernity, when it eventually began arriving there. In the early 1990s, when I revisited the village where I spent many of my childhood summers, I was aghast to see standard-issue prefab houses standing side by side with the beautifully painted and decorated old wooden dwellings. Then I chastised myself for my aesthetic snobbery. It was understandable why the villagers felt proud of their newly achieved modernity, and I think Miłosz, who was so aware of technological change, with its positive as well as destructive results, would not have begrudged them their newfound comforts.

In his autobiography, *Native Realm*, Miłosz introduces the place from which he came in different terms. Starting with a particular moment and object—"an old chest painted green with red flowers and a similarly painted canopy bed," which he discovers in an attic of a Swiss home on Lake Geneva and which had been passed on among generations of its inhabitants, through centuries of stability—he goes on to say that in order to explain what this object meant to him, he "would have to go back, arduously, to the very beginning and entangle myself in dates, histories, of institutions, battles and customs" that rendered such continuity impossible. In other words, he would have to explain where he came from: the Other Europe. "Undoubtedly I could call Europe my home," he says, "but it was a home that refused to acknowledge itself as a whole; instead, as if on the strength of some self-imposed taboo, it classified its population into two categories: members of the family . . . and poor relations."

Later, in introducing a chapter called "City of My Youth," he strikes a note of more explicit resentment on behalf of that underestimated place: "I see an injustice," he writes. "A Parisian does not have to bring his city out of nothingness every time he wants to describe it. A wealth of allusions lies at his disposal, for his city exists in works of word, brush and chisel. . . . But I, returning in thought to the streets where the most important part of my life unfolded, am obliged to invent the most utilitarian sort of symbols."

Native Realm could be read as one of the most impersonal autobiographies ever written, but that would be to misunderstand what for Miłosz (as perhaps for all of us, if we were sufficiently cognizant of it) constitutes "the personal." In a sense, the whole book—and, indeed, much of his oeuvre—is an attempt to evoke and explain to a Western reader the multiple meanings of "the Other Europe": the realm that defined him and that remained largely unknown, or at best imagined as inferior, obscure, and altogether insignificant by the inhabitants of what was considered Europe *tout court:* Europe, which stood for civilization itself. In a sense, coming from that "Other" place—and especially with Miłosz's acute awareness of its marginality—is a position similar to that of an immigrant or an exile: it increases the awareness that our familiar world, our versions of personality, our deepest assumptions about existence, are not the only version of "the human."

Almost from the beginning, and certainly as he began to travel in his youth, Miłosz was deeply conscious of the extent to which he was shaped by particular circumstances and by impersonal or transpersonal forces: history, language, religion, culture. As it happened, the city in which he grew up—known today as Vilnius—was, during the interwar period, one of the fascinating metropolises of Europe: multinational, multireligious, multilingual, and known then by several slightly different names: Wilno, Vilnius, Wilna. It was also a complicated place to explain. Miłosz was born on June 30, 1911; when he was a child, Vilnius and the bucolic parts of Lithuania he described often in his writing were located within the Russian Empire; before that, they belonged to the Polish-Lithuanian Commonwealth, until this formation was partitioned by the neighboring empires in 1795; in 1918, however, Poland regained its nationhood, and Lithuania declared independence from the new country. But even then, Vilnius remained a city of several religious and ethnic groups—Lithuanian, Jewish, Polish, Belorussian—that coexisted in various states of amity, indifference, and, with the rise of interwar ethno-nationalism, increasing hostility, directed particularly against the Jews. Miłosz came from a Polish-speaking, Polish-identified family that belonged to the minor nobility, and he was initiated into Catholicism early on, through its rituals and traditions, and later through formal education. He was also, from early on, highly aware of the Jewish presence and culture in the city. He knew that Vilnius was known as the "Jerusalem of the north," for its famous yeshivas and rabbinical scholarship; when he began writing poetry, he was drawn to Jewish groups, because they were largely secular and nonconformist. During one of the anti-Semitic attacks that were becoming more frequent at his university, he was apparently the only one to come to the aid of his fellow Jewish students.

For Miłosz, aside from potent early experiences, aspects of his thought and attitude toward the world were seeded by his formal studies, which he never entirely abandoned. A visitor from western Europe to interwar Vilnius might have been surprised by the high caliber of education offered in its schools in the interwar period. Miłosz's intellectual formation was powerful—and it was the stratum underlying much of his later thought, even as he rebelled against some aspects of it. He engaged in a complicated internal dialogue with the dour teacher who provided his religious instruction in the principles of Catholicism, and who brought to his lessons a dark sense of humor and a propensity to emphasize sins of the flesh. As a fiery, youthfully purist adolescent, Miłosz was particularly repelled by what might be called "organized religion," and he seethed at the spectacle of "good society" at the Sunday services that pupils in his school had to attend, and the hypocrisy he sensed in its members. He discovered only later, he says, that such feelings were called "hatred of the bourgeoisie"— an attitude he came to reject, together with the idea of judging people on the basis of their group identity.

The intellectual intensity—even anguish—the young Miłosz brought to religious questions was as impressive as the questions he posed (how can cruelty be justified in a God-governed world; why should humans be more important than animals; how is eternity to be understood, given the time line of evolution). But whatever his doubts about the beliefs and practices of formal Catholicism, his conviction that we need a basic morality—

and that the ability to distinguish between right and wrong is what distinguishes human nature from the rest of nature—never abandoned him, and it led him to grapple with questions of faith, and its collective loss, throughout his long life. He was attracted early on to the "heresies" he studied in a church manual—especially Manicheanism, in which the polarity between good and evil was attributed to human choice, rather than higher forces. Indeed, one of Miłosz's objections to formal Catholicism—at least as it was taught during his high school years—was that its morality was collective rather than individual and that it did not foster a sense of responsibility toward particular people. This was perhaps particularly true of Polish Catholicism, which, he notes, was closely entangled with national identity, especially after Poland was partitioned in the last quarter of the eighteenth century and ceased to exist as a country for almost a 150 years. The question of the Other Europe has a long historical derivation.

Yet while his education led Miłosz to wrestle with questions of human ethics, it is one of the interesting revelations of his autobiography that, during his high school years, he was "drawn to the science laboratory, with its modern microscopes, as to a workshop of learning that was the least abstract because it related to my experiences of hunting and walking in the forest." While still in high school, he delivered a talk on Darwin and natural selection, and among all his religious and intellectual doubts, he says he had "no doubts about one thing: my future profession of naturalist was settled."

Of course, it wasn't settled at all—but much of his poetry springs from his love of nature and is permeated by his close knowledge of it. In addition, Miłosz's Vilnius education included elements more directly relevant to the practice of poetry. His training in Latin classics and translation instilled in him a basic but crucial lesson that "what one says changes, depending upon how one says it," and also the hard-earned conviction, conveyed by a demanding teacher, that "perfection is worth the effort . . . in other words, he showed us how to respect literature as the fruit of arduous labor." To see writing as arduous labor, rather than an outpouring of some creative genius, would have appealed to Miłosz greatly; the value of such labor is one of the threads that runs through all his writing. "Bureaucracy is parasitic because its activities are unproductive," he observed caustically about his brief prewar period of office work. "They do not shape matter." And he went on to say, "The peasant is honest because his energy is transformed into bread. The artisan is honest because he makes over wood, hide, or metal." The energy of labor is what converts stone into cathedrals, plants into food, steel into bridges, perceptions into understanding—and words into poetry.

Other leitmotifs that make their appearance in his student years can be traced throughout his work. He tells us that for his final high school examination, he wrote an essay on the "river of time," for which, he adds in a rare note of self-praise, "my paper received the highest mark." His reasons for choosing the subject were highly philosophical. "I was stirred by the mystery of universal movement," he says, "where all things are linked together, are interdependent, create one another, transcend one another, where nothing conforms to rigid definitions." For a high school senior, this is a sophisticated and, indeed, a prescient idea, which scientists continue to grapple with today. In Miłosz's work, "movement"—of history, of the cosmos, of nature and evolution, of technological development, and, above all, of human time—becomes one of the deep themes woven into the fabric of both his poetic and essayistic reflections. Here's an early poem called "Encounter," written in Vilnius in 1936:

> We were riding through frozen fields in a
>   wagon at dawn.
> A red wing rose in the darkness.

And suddenly a hare ran across the road.
One of us pointed to it with his hand.

That was long ago. Today neither of them is
     alive,
Not the hare, nor the man who made the
     gesture.

O my love, where are they, where are they
     going
The flash of a hand, streak of movement,
     rustle of pebbles.
I ask not out of sorrow, but in wonder.

A moment; a streak of movement; and the sheer
poignancy—and wonder—of ordinary loss, of
passing moments, the passage of time itself. Such
motifs will recur throughout his poetry, although
later they will become inflected by much darker
contexts.

   After that early intention to become a naturalist, however, Miłosz did not arrive at a poetic
vocation immediately. It was perhaps part of his
attempt to maintain an inner balance—not to in-
dulge his inclinations or ambitions too easily—
that in college, despite his already strong literary
proclivities, he studied law. "If I rightly understand the motives for my choice," he says, "I was
guided by an exaggerated fear that if I revealed
what I wanted to become too early, I would bring

down defeat upon myself." Perhaps to declare himself "a poet" might have seemed presumptuous and pretentious. "At the same time," he adds, "some instinct whispered that literature should not feed on itself but should be supported by a knowledge of society." That instinct enriched all his writing, and when he was still a student, it may have accounted for his ambivalent attraction to aspects of Marxism—as well as his eventual repulsion against its rigidities. During his university years, groups of all political stripes were active among students in Vilnius, and their politics were taken seriously. This was a period when students not only discussed politics but participated in them. Miłosz wasn't wholeheartedly drawn to any of the groups, but for a young person of temperamentally liberal inclinations at a time of rising right-wing extremism, Marxism was the preferable—really, the default—option. It was also unavoidable: in the air, part of the climate of opinion. Miłosz, with his complicated view of Russian sensibility (he thought Russian poetry was too musical by half) and his more concrete suspicions of rising Soviet communism, was not a natural recruit for Marxist activism; yet, interestingly, he was also afraid of a tendency in himself, which a critic of his early student poems called his desire "to keep clean hands." In other words, young Miłosz understood that a desire for moral purity which led to avoidance of action and commitment could also be a moral fault.

For a while, Miłosz tried participating in a Marxist group and "bellowed" rousing speeches. Eventually, however, he revolted against the sloganeering simplifications of Marxist student politics and the need to falsify himself in order to profess its beliefs. At the same time, he never lost his need for large frameworks of perception and understanding—for a morality and a metaphysics; and as he turned from politics to poetry, he developed what might be called a metaphysics of particularity. The sources of meaning, he felt, are to be found in particular attachments and perceptions. But the need to understand one person or creature fully leads, in turn, to questions about the underpinnings of life: the riddle of consciousness, the sources of happiness, why anything is rather than otherwise; and it seems to me that this double movement gives much of his poetry its unique combination of sensuous vividness and sometimes austere, cerebral music—the music of thought.

Perhaps what Miłosz was really abandoning as he turned away from Marxism was the lure of ideological systems altogether. Instead, he joined the poetic circles in Vilnius that were, to his pleasure, nonconformist and multicultural; the presence of Jewish poets in these groupings was something he particularly enjoyed. Miłosz's affinity for Jewish culture—perhaps for Jewish nonnationalist sensibility—was clearly authentic and expressed itself in many ways: in his friendships, in his poetry, and eventually in learning Hebrew so that he could translate the Old Testament. Nevertheless, in *Native Realm*, he says that writing about the Jewish population of Vilnius in retrospect is "hard" for him, "because no small effort is demanded if one is to distinguish these pre-war tensions from one of the greatest tragedies of history: the slaughter of some three million 'non-Aryan' Polish citizens by the Nazis." His account of interethnic relations in prewar Vilnius—and particularly the prevailing attitudes toward the Jewish part of the population—sometimes shows signs of that anguish; but it is also an impressive attempt to do justice, as much as possible in a few compressed pages, to all the groups and their collective attitudes, in what was then an uneasily multicultural society. He fully acknowledges the strong strain of anti-Semitism among the Catholic, highly nationalistic Poles, and its sources not only in prejudice but in sheer ignorance and a comprehensive misunderstanding of Jewish culture and sensibility. The misunderstandings extended especially to the newly secularized, middle-class Jews who, in contrast to Orthodox Jews, with their particular garb and use of Yiddish or Hebrew, were almost indistinguishable from their Polish counterparts. (Among Poland's newly secularized Jewish population were, quite astoundingly, several of the country's leading poets.)

But in his account of cross-ethnic relations, Miłosz also conscientiously notes elements of Jewish attitudes that constituted a kind of provocation: the pro-Russian or pro-Soviet tendencies quite prevalent among younger Jews; economic as well as intellectual and professional competition between two poor populations, which allowed some Jewish businessmen to thrive rather more than their non-Jewish counterparts; and, in another vein, the disproportionate predominance of Jewish students at some universities, especially in the fields of law and medicine.

I can only admire Miłosz's sensitivity and his courage in writing about such matters. The awareness of the Holocaust, so present for him, makes it indeed extremely difficult to speak about the Polish-Jewish relations that preceded it from any perspective, including a Jewish one—as I discovered when I wrote on this subject myself, from my more "legitimate" position as the daughter of Holocaust survivors. Our knowledge of the terrible culmination is hard to disentangle from what went on before. But history is not like story, leading to a predetermined end; and there is perhaps no history more complex—or more fascinating—than that of Polish Jews and of Polish-Jewish relations during the long centuries of their co-existence. Beginning with the eleventh century, Poland had the largest Jewish population of any country in Europe and the largest percentage of Jewish inhabitants in the world. It also presented all the varieties of what was really multicultur-alism *avant la lettre,* with phases of amity and enmity, of virtual self-governance for the Jewish minority, and fierce prejudice against it. It is a history that until recently was almost entirely unknown in the Western world and remains a poorly understood and highly contentious subject even today.

Eventually, Miłosz acquired knowledge of society and its workings in the most informative and most demanding way: through direct expe-rience. But his early poetry also emerged from a different and very potent source—an attitude, or a complex of feelings and sensations he referred to as "pansexuality"; that is, an avid, powerful attraction to all forms of life, to na-ture, humans, places, landscapes. "My erotic de-sire went further than any object," he writes. "My pansexuality included the whole world and, not able to be a god or an ogre who swallows the world, tastes it with his tongue, bites, I could only take it in an embrace with my eyes. Besides, like all hungers, this one disperses, too, at the limit of words."

A limit he tries again and again to break through precisely in words, and through words. Especially, of course, in poetry, which can do more than describe the object itself; it can express the hunger Miłosz felt and the compelling sensuality of the visible world.

"Pansexuality," with its wonder at the actually existing, Edenic world, was also a philosophy of specificity rather than generalization; the conviction that meaning resides in—or, rather, begins with—what Miłosz eventually called "the immense call of the Particular": the singular person, the domestic, mundane detail, the momentary encounter, the ordinary and the concrete. This was a conviction that never deserted him and that, together with the immense cargo of knowledge he carried within himself, gives his poetry, through the many dramatic changes of circumstance in his life, its inexhaustible fuel and its understated, complex music: the music of wonder and of thought.

▧ Between student years and exile, and before the great and grim lessons of History, there was, for Miłosz, exploration of the actually existing world—particularly the part of it that to a large extent then stood for "the World" itself: western Europe.

The early 1930s were, for Miłosz and his friends, a time of adventurous student journeys, by train (a "dishonest" method of transport) and canoe (honest, but at times very dangerous). In 1931 he embarked on such a journey with two fellow members of the "Vagabonds Club," nicknamed Robespierre and Elephant. (Interestingly, the habit of giving nicknames to close friends persists in Poland till today. I'm not sure I have an explanation for this cultural epiphenomenon—but perhaps it is an expression of the playful intimacy that has always been part of the Polish ethos of friendship and has persisted despite and within all the larger conflicts.) Such personal details aside, Miłosz was clearly very aware, as he set out on his westward trip, that he was coming from a part of the world seen (if it was seen at all) as less civilized, less cultured, less advanced in every way.

Moreover, despite his deep attachment to the regions of his childhood and youth, Miłosz to some extent shared this preconception, and his discovery of the West was a complex education. As the three friends begin their journey in the nearest country of Czechoslovakia, he admires the cleanliness and neatness of its small towns and the liveliness of Prague, even then thronged by tourists—"the first Western European capital I saw," he writes. (The fact that he places Czechoslovakia in the West prefigures later arguments about nomenclature, and the claim—put forward most passionately by Milan Kundera—that several countries of the Other Europe should be seen as belonging to "central" as opposed to "eastern" Europe.)

But on that prewar journey, there were also more startling, and more disillusioning, moments. On a bridge near the French border, the three friends saw a sign raised up so as to be easily visible to various unwary travelers, which "prohibited Gypsies, Poles, Rumanians, and Bulgarians from entering the country." "France, our spiritual sister, welcomed us," Miłosz comments ironically. One can imagine the young explorers' shock; indeed, even in long retrospect, such crude expressions of bigotry don't fit into the idea of France, which for so many stood for civilization itself. Was this a reaction against the influx of immigrants in great numbers? The 1930s—the years of the Great Depression—were also a decade of mass migrations from eastern to western Europe, in an era before the Iron Curtain made such border crossings virtually impossible; and this spawned its share of extreme reactions, including the rise of fascism—however indiscernible it might have been from afar.

Nevertheless, even after this disconcerting beginning, the three young travelers fell into a state of full enchantment once they reached Paris. Mind you, who could help it? The first encounter with that city has stunned many into helpless aesthetic submission.

Miłosz stayed in Paris for a year, studying on a scholarship arranged by a distinguished if distant relative, Oscar de Lubicz Milosz, a diplomat and poet who was also a Swedenborgian mystic, and who remained a powerful and formative influence on his young protégé throughout his life.

During that initial sojourn, Miłosz came to admire France not only for the beauty of its architecture or the palpable presence of the past in its cities, but also for its love of individual freedom and the respect for privacy that allowed people to live out their lives as they wished. Coming from a culture where the price of closer human relations was a greater intrusiveness, young Miłosz might well have wanted such freedom for himself. Indeed, in his writing, where he could exercise control over what he wanted to reveal and conceal, he protected his privacy quite punctiliously for many years.

But in France itself, as their stay went on, Miłosz and his travel companions became painfully aware of the dramatic social contrasts prevailing there, and the indifference, behind those privately closed doors, to the suffering of others—especially the "tragic mass" of the impoverished and the unemployed, among whom migrant Poles were very prominent. "We were sensitive to the smell of misery and brutality," Miłosz writes, and he returns to the theme in a moving poem called "Ballad of Levallois," whose rare explanatory subtitle notes that it refers to "barracks for the unemployed, Levallois-Perret, 1935":

> O God, have mercy on Levallois,
> Look under these chestnut trees poisoned
>   with smoke,
> Give a moment of joy to the weak and the
>   drunk,
> O God, have mercy on Levallois. . . .
>
> All day long they stole and cursed,
> Now they lie in their bunks and lick their
>   wounds,
> And while the darkness thickens over Paris
> They hide their faces in their thieving
>   hands.
> O God, have mercy on Levallois. . . .

It was they who lifted you above themselves,
Their hands sculpted your face.
So deign to look on your faithful priests,
Give them the joys of table and bed.

The poem springs from the same source as the later prose observations on this subject in *Native Realm*, but in "Ballad," the sense of outrage young Miłosz felt at the misery he saw in France is heightened both by the understated lyricism of the verse and the sacrilegious form of the prayer—a defiant appeal to God on behalf of the drunk, the thieving, the utterly miserable, and the worker-priests who sculpted the many beautiful images of divinity in Paris's cathedrals. Miłosz's sensitivity to human misery was indeed deep, and his enchantment with the magical West didn't entirely survive, or was at least greatly modified by that first, youthful encounter with its actualities.

◈ Miłosz returned to France much later, in very different circumstances—and his first response was a newly inflected sense of wonder. "Today, the most amazing thing about Paris for me is that it still exists," he wrote in the late 1950s.

Undoubtedly, this perhaps surprising sense of surprise also derives from Miłosz's vantage point in the Other Europe. Between his very different sojourns in Paris, there was the Event that changed everything, changed it utterly, and that bisected the entire twentieth century into "before" and "after." This was, of course, World War II, and while this global conflict had awful consequences for all the countries of Europe, it was particularly cruel in the eastern parts of it—and most catastrophically destructive in Poland itself. Between 1939 and 1945, Poland was the epicenter not of one but two violent upheavals: the Nazi war of occupation and conquest against the Poles, during which three million people lost their lives; and the project of extermination directed against the Jews, and perpetrated largely on Polish territory, in which three million Polish Jews, or 90 percent of the prewar Jewish population of Poland, were murdered. And while Paris was physically saved by the Vichy government's collusion with the Germans, the Nazi invasion and occupation of Poland reduced Warsaw to rubble and ruin, killing, among all those unbearable, anonymous numbers, many of Miłosz's friends.

Miłosz lived through most of the hellish years in Warsaw—that is, in one of the inferno's deepest circles. His movements at the beginning of the conflict were complicated, but shortly after the bombardment of Warsaw at the outbreak of the war, he decided, together with many others, to escape eastward, out of the zone of greatest danger, and make his way to the Ukrainian city of Lviv (as it is now known). This is what he writes in *Native Realm* about one of the revelations brought about by that experience: "I could reduce all that happened to me then to a few things. Lying in the field near a highway bombarded by airplanes, I riveted my eyes on a stone and two blades of grass in front of me. Listening to the whistle of a bomb, I suddenly understood the value of matter: that stone and those two blades of grass formed a whole kingdom, an infinity of forms, shades, textures, lights. They were the universe. I had always refused to accept the division into macro- and micro-cosmos; I preferred to contemplate a piece of bark or a bird's wing rather than sunsets or sunrises. But now I saw into the depths of matter with exceptional intensity."

The epiphany is of course consistent with his entire vision: his desire to grasp the essence of things; his belief that meaning inheres in the concrete and the particular and proceeds from it to deeper understanding. But given the circumstances in which it takes place, his description of the terrifying experience is almost eerily impersonal. Perhaps it is possible to understand his detachment as something that happens in moments of great danger: a kind of absenting of yourself from yourself, standing beside or outside or even above yourself, which has been described by many people who have faced a deadly threat.

But the detachment captured by that description characterizes almost all of Miłosz's writing about that catastrophic time. Almost—not all. That, I think, is important. Nevertheless, the determination to maintain moral and intellectual equilibrium, the refusal of excessive emotion or sentimentality in the midst of the most wrenching circumstances, is the main tone of his wartime recollections. After that first escape, Miłosz decided to make his way back to Warsaw, partly to rejoin his future wife, Janka; but that plan was complicated by the Soviet invasion of Poland from the east brought about by the Molotov-Ribbentrop Pact, and then by the Soviet invasion of Lithuania. It was a dangerous journey, during which even the most terrifying moments of physical danger "did not ruffle a deep-seated indifference, a self-forgetfulness that could perhaps better be described as the sensitivity of a camera, ready to register everything that is visible." An indifference that was also, he implies, a form of freedom—after all, there was nothing to do but live for the day and experience the here and now.

Miłosz maintained this state throughout most of the cataclysm. He realized, better than most, that he was living through a "total war" and in the center of its most vicious ravages; and yet he can write, "Its cruelties are not interesting." Instead, he interweaves an account of his time in occupied Warsaw with rarely encountered modes of analysis. It was clear from the outset, he says, that from the German point of view the invasion of Poland was a mistake—a waste of resources, doomed to failure, and he attributes this mistake to a mechanistic view of history. "In a sense, Hitler took Darwinism, 'the struggle for existence' and the 'survival of the fittest' too seriously, and by identifying history with nature he ignored the limits of blind force." The Nazis were "too inferior intellectually to go beyond vulgarized biology." Again, this fits indirectly into Miłosz's fundamental assumptions, his sense that humans are not merely biological, and that they are possessed of an intrinsic morality—unless they are, as the Nazis were in his view, moral idiots. But still, for someone of his analytic powers, the diagnosis is very strange. Surely, however sordid it was, and whatever horrors it led to, it is difficult to see Nazi "vulgarized biology" (Miłosz is clearly thinking here about the idea of "inferior races") as "an intellectual" mistake; and surely, however intellectually sordid he may have been, Hitler was all too methodical in his uses of brute power.

Was this, too, an attempt to remain disengaged in the face of overwhelming horror—and danger? And perhaps to do so by maintaining a sense of intellectual superiority over what was, in fact, cruelly superior force? In one of his sharp paradoxes, Miłosz notes that in occupied Warsaw there was complete freedom of thought, "precisely because National Socialism was an intellectual zero." In other words, he didn't have to grapple with its ideas or take a position on it, as he felt compelled to do, for example, with Marxism. Still, he was perfectly aware that his survival was not at all assured, and that in order to be really free, he "had to solve the problem of hope, or, rather, to find a position from which hope and despair were equally irrelevant."

This is stoicism worthy of Seneca or, rather, going far beyond him. Yet Miłosz managed to retain emotional distance from the horrors of the wartime years—and particularly from the turmoil of Polish resistance politics—almost until the end of the war. Not that he was uninvolved in underground activities as the carnage went on, but his main interest was in working on his poetry—which, he thought, would have to search for new forms and modes of expression to measure up to the cataclysm. With Janka's help, he participated actively in underground publishing—regular publishing of any kind was forbidden during the Nazi occupation—and sold what may have been the earliest literary volume of poetry in wartime Poland. Altogether, forbidden cultural activity defiantly thrived in occupied Warsaw. Miłosz took part in what must have been heady discussions of essays he and other literati wrote on philosophical aspects of literature. He was part of an actors' group that, he says, put on excellent performances. And he obtained a job in a library, an institution that had been salvaged through an elaborate ruse to deceive the Nazi authorities, although it was not open to the public. In this position, Miłosz could read to his heart's content, and he also used the time to learn English, claiming that his meditations on English poetry— particularly that of T. S. Eliot—helped him reach "deeper layers" in his own poetry. In another vein, he translated *As You Like It*, noting that "bucolic Shakespeare proved to be first-rate therapy."

I wonder if the "deeper layers" led him to an almost childlike simplicity evident in a series of poems called *The World*, published in 1943. Several of the poems include the figure of "the Father" explaining the world to his children—the world as it should be and as Miłosz continued to understand it—containing simple but ultimately mysterious forms of Being. Here are a few lines from a poem titled "Faith":

> Faith is in you whenever you look
> At a dewdrop or a floating leaf
> And know that they are because they have
> to be.

And from another, called "Hope":

> Hope is with you when you believe
> The earth is not a dream but living flesh,
> That sight, touch, and hearing do not lie,
> That all things you have ever seen here
> Are like a garden looked at from a gate.

Are there echoes of T. S. Eliot's *Four Quartets* and his rose garden here? But unlike Eliot, Miłosz could not spend all his time in Warsaw in poetic meditation. He had to fend for himself and Janka; and he mentions, not without satisfaction, that he engaged (successfully!) in illicit trade of cigarettes and whisky. He also participated in activities of a cunning enterprise called the Firm (after MI5?)—an intriguing outfit that, under the cover of Nazi authorization, engaged in profitable currency trade and, in addition, used forged documents to save Jewish lives by spiriting people out of Warsaw to safer places.

Improbable as it may seem, the Firm also delivered first-rate, devil-may-care entertainment in the midst of deepening gloom and danger. Miłosz mentions that the music at one of its meetings was provided by "two of Poland's best composers, Lutosławski and Panufnik . . . playing on two pianos"—a bit of incidental information that I find moving and, actually, quite astonishing. Witold Lutosławski and Andrzej Panufnik went on to gain worldwide fame after the war as part of Poland's musical new wave, and it is stirring to think of them and other artists, poets, and intellectuals defying all risks to practice their art in the besieged city. It also seems to me that the composers' presence at underground events throws light on Polish postwar modernism and its crucial differences from the music of, say, Boulez or Stockhausen. The difference—I think we can see in retrospect—is that the powerful music of Polish composers was informed not only by the desire to experiment with new forms but by the experience of extremity and of human tragedy.

In Miłosz's own canon—and the canon of wartime literature altogether—two poems are exceptional for several reasons. These are "Campo dei Fiori" and "A Poor Christian Looks at the Ghetto," both of which were written in 1943, as the Warsaw Ghetto uprising was taking place, and are therefore among the earliest—if not the first—literary responses to the Holocaust by a nonparticipant in that dark event.

"Campo dei Fiori" came out of an actual experience or, rather, moment of perception. Miłosz was in a tramway that stopped, for a lengthy time, right near the wall separating the Warsaw Ghetto from the rest of Warsaw. Outside the wall, there was a carousel on which people were enjoying a beautiful spring evening. From within the ghetto walls, shots of the doomed uprising were loudly heard. In the poem, Miłosz compares this juxtaposition to the burning of Giordano Bruno in Campo dei Fiori, where people were filling up the taverns "before the flames had died." In a much later conversation, Miłosz said that he wrote "Campo dei Fiori" immediately after witnessing this sight. The wrenching irony of the poem comes from the spectators' utter indifference to the tragedy unfolding in such close proximity—but behind an existential as well as a concrete barrier created by the ghetto's enclosure. Miłosz clearly understood the wound of that indifference—particularly for those inmates of the ghetto for whom Poles had been, until recently, colleagues, neighbors, sometimes friends. Poignant entries in diaries written by the ghetto's inmates speak about sights of normal life visible outside, in the streets of Warsaw, while the people inside were consigned to a nether realm of unspeakable suffering and almost certain death. So near, and yet so terribly far.

"A Poor Christian Looks at the Ghetto" is a more severe and perhaps more profound feat of metaphoric thought, imagining an underworld of the dead:

> Slowly, boring a tunnel, a guardian mole makes his way,
> With a small red lamp fastened to his forehead.
> He touches buried bodies, counts them, pushes on,
> He distinguishes human ashes by their luminous vapor,
> The ashes of each man by a different part of the spectrum.
> Bees build around a red trace.
> Ants build around the place left by my body.
>
> I am afraid, so afraid of the guardian mole.
> He has swollen eyelids, like a Patriarch
> Who has sat much in the light of candles
> Reading the great book of the species.
>
> What will I tell him, I, a Jew of the New Testament,
> Waiting two thousand years for the second coming of Jesus?

My broken body will deliver me to his sight
And he will count me among the helpers of
     death:
The uncircumcised.

"Campo dei Fiori" is a moving feat of imaginative empathy, but the uncanny metaphors of "A Poor Christian"—the poem's descent into an eerily imagined underworld—suggest, in a sense, a fuller identification with the Other. The dread and guilt so potently expressed are possible because the poet is fully aware that judgment will be leveled by a Jewish patriarch to whose verdict he, as a Christian, has to submit. But the poem is also prophetic in its faith in the powers of memory: its intuition that no matter how deeply the evidence of extermination is buried, the identity of each victim, and the evidence of the killers' actions, will be retrieved even from the ashes.

Memory, for good reason, became one of Miłosz's master concepts in the aftermath of the war. But when I first read Miłosz's two poems about the event that later came to be named the Holocaust, I felt not only amazement at the leap of the poet's imagination but a kind of gratitude: here, the extent and dreadful nature of the Jewish tragedy was fully recognized, and recognition is perhaps the only form of reparation—the only redress possible—after enormous and irreversible wrongs have been committed.

Is the poem also a confession of remorse, or even a kind of collective guilt for being "among the helpers of death" by virtue of being Christian? Objectively, Miłosz and his brother Andrzej did more, much more than most non-Jewish Poles, to help their Jewish countrymen at a time of ultimate danger. Both were involved in the hazardous activity of helping Jewish people find hiding places and in sheltering them; eventually, both were honored by Yad Vashem in Israel as the Righteous Among Nations. But in his recollections, Miłosz speaks about such activities very little, and only in relation to his "cowardly" fear of dangerous situations. Here, the restraint seems to be an impressive instance of what he called his "moral scrupulosity": to say more would have been to boast, or perhaps to exaggerate the hazards he risked, in the face of greater suffering.

But if Miłosz is mostly silent about such matters in his reminiscences, that is perhaps also because the inevitably tormented emotions in the face of horror that came to be seen as "unimaginable" and "unspeakable" can be more fully expressed in poetry. He may well have felt that the unfolding Holocaust was an event too dark for ordinary sympathy—or for a forthright declaration of attitude.

The two poems are among the most famous poems in Miłosz's canon, and they carry a particular meaning for me—as they do for many others—for personal as well as historical reasons. My parents both lived through the Holocaust in a tiny shtetl in what was then the Polish part of Ukraine. Their lives were saved with the help of some Polish, and mostly Ukrainian, neighbors, but their entire families—parents, siblings, cousins—were murdered by the Nazis. When I eventually wrote about this and the larger history of Polish-Jewish relations in my book *Shtetl*, I was doing so, inevitably, from the Jewish side of the equation—but not entirely. I was, through language and cultural formation, both Polish and Jewish. (I liked the formulation suggested by the modernist poet Aleksander Wat, one of Miłosz's close friends, who answered questions about his identity by saying that he was "Polish-Polish, and Jewish-Jewish.") From that double perspective, I felt acutely the difficulty of writing about that history's darkest chapter, and I could well imagine that from Miłosz's non-Jewish vantage point, and with his sensitivity to such issues, the subject might have seemed untouchable as well as—

except through the multivalent suggestiveness of poetry—unspeakable.

Miłosz would have undoubtedly felt that his criticism of attitudes adopted by the Polish underground, and his complicated feelings of revolt and detachment from the Polish catastrophe, were something to which he had a fuller right. Indeed, he retained his critical distance from events even—or especially—in relation to the Warsaw Uprising: that audacious and doomed attempt to defeat the Nazis through armed resistance, which for Poland was the culminating tragedy of the war. Miłosz was not among the approximately 45,000 people who volunteered to join the effort, and his reasons were, not surprisingly, complicated. "There would be no point today in trying to convince myself or others that I had any sort of talent for heroism," he writes (whether in a spirit of self-deprecation or acknowledgment, it is hard to tell). Undoubtedly, the decision to join the uprising required a degree of courage that really was heroic. But for Miłosz, there were also more political considerations. In *Native Realm*, he acknowledges that Poland produced the largest resistance movement of any occupied country, against the longest odds—and that it was "self-sacrificing as perhaps no other in Europe." And yet, he says, he felt no temptation to join the uprising—not only for personal reasons, but because he was restrained by "passionate hostility to the leaders of the Home Army" who led the non-Communist resistance movement throughout the war. He thought they were intellectually inferior and showed rightist tendencies, not only in the conduct of the resistance but in their vision of the country's future. Miłosz was reinforced in these convictions by a dialectically skilled philosopher-poet nicknamed "Tiger" who was an intellectual interlocutor and mentor throughout the war, and for whom "living well" at a time of catastrophe meant "not sinning in thought against the structure of the universe, which is meaningful." In other words, respecting reason and meaningful thought was more important than impetuous action.

But the poems sometimes tell a different story. Here are some fragments from "Café," signed Warsaw, 1944, which prefigures, at that early moment, the poetry of memory and witness so central to Miłosz's later oeuvre:

Of those at the table in the café
where on winter noons a garden of frost
    glittered on windowpanes
I alone survived.
I could go in there if I wanted to
and drumming my fingers in a chilly void
convoke shadows. . . .

Sometimes when the evening aurora paints
the roofs in a poor street
and I contemplate the sky, I see in the white
clouds
a table wobbling. The waiter whirls with his
tray
and they look at me with a burst of laughter
for I still don't know what it is to die at the
hand of man,
they know—they know it well.

The guilt and the shame of survival here are expressed through the terrible mockery of the poet by the dead; on reading this, I feel acutely that I have no right to pass judgment on Miłosz's attitudes toward the uprising from my perspective "after." Nevertheless, I must admit that, given the extent of the tragedy unfolding around him, his resolve to maintain distance from increasingly agonizing events (if we are to believe the explicit language of prose in his reminiscences) strikes me as verging on a kind of denial. A denial of what? He writes about two epiphanies—at the outset of the war and toward its end, and both have to do with hatred of prewar Poland and all its institutions, its bureaucratic structures (for which he had nothing but scorn), its "subtle collective censorship" and its "latest pathetic and messianic embodiment"—namely, the Warsaw

Uprising, which he summarizes as a "blamewor-thy, lightheaded enterprise . . . although two hun-dred thousand corpses do carry weight, and no one can tell what shapes the legend may take."

Was I, in my Polish education, brought up on "the legend" of the uprising? I don't think so, but the events of the war were hardly abstract history for my postwar generation. I grew up in Poland so shortly after the cataclysm, and in such geo-graphic proximity to its greatest destruction, that, like many children who came into the world in its close aftermath, I felt that it was my true origin; that, in a sense, I came *from* the war. The signs and scars of destruction were every-where visible: in men with missing limbs; in the orphaned children whose faces emanated a great sadness; in the ruins of Warsaw, with its rubble and ruined buildings, which formed my early store of indelible and never forgotten im-agery. There were low-voiced rumors about a neighbor who had been a resistance fighter and was probably suffering from what was not yet understood as PTSD; later, I learned of others who were imprisoned and tortured by the Soviet-sponsored regime.

These were, during the Iron Curtain decades, censored and forbidden subjects—as was the subject of the Holocaust itself. But forcibly sup-pressed memories eventually reemerged with redoubled force. It was only in the early twenty-first century—after Poland had undergone several dramatic changes of governance—that I learned more fully about the uprising itself, in the course of visiting a recently opened museum in Warsaw dedicated to that event. The museum includes recorded recollections of participants in the uprising, many of whom were still in their adolescence when they decided to join the battle—and the anguished conversations with their parents, who feared for their children's lives but didn't want to stop them from following their conscience. I learned about the astonishing effort to keep Warsaw from starvation; to bring information to the city's inhabitants (which involved the participation of numerous women); to save, even as people were dying in great numbers, as much of the capital's cultural heritage as possible; and to fight, with pitifully limited means, the superior force of Nazi weaponry. There are recordings of speeches by Stalin, who encouraged the uprising to begin—and who then ordered the Soviet army to wait on the other side of the Vistula River, while the Germans proceeded with their carnage and reduced Warsaw to utter rubble before retreating. This allowed Stalin's army to march into the ruined city unopposed and to begin the political takeover of Poland, which was soon after formally relegated to the Soviet sphere by the Yalta agreement. Exact numbers of the dead are hard to ascertain, but between 150,000 and 200,000 people died in that terrible culmination of the war. In retrospect, it is clear that the uprising—led by a government-in-exile in London—was ill-timed. Today there are historians who think it was a necessary act of resistance, and those who think it was a terrible mistake with incalculable costs. There are yet others—and I find it hard not to agree with them—who believe there were no good choices to be made: a situation that is the very essence of tragedy.

Still, for Miłosz, if we are to believe his own later testimony, the most important concern throughout the war years remained the development of his poetry, and he felt, toward the end, that he achieved a kind of breakthrough both in formal and personal ways. He abandoned his attempts to write "pure" poetry or poetry on specifically "social" themes. "Only now," he writes, "had the contradiction vanished. Now even the most personal poem translated a human situation and contained a streak of irony that made it objective."

Extreme circumstances capture the individual in a collective net. Miłosz always resisted such capture, but I confess that the word "objective" strikes me as strange here. Indeed, Miłosz's autobiographical account of the war years—

although, to reiterate, I feel acutely that I have no right to pass judgment on it—is the one instance in his vast oeuvre in which I find his determination to retain his distance from events excessive, and not entirely convincing.

Nor, clearly, was it complete, and there are telling moments when the detachment could not hold. Here is an excerpt from a piercingly poignant poem called "In Warsaw," written in 1945:

You swore never to be
A ritual mourner.
You swore never to touch
The deep wounds of your nation
So you would not make them holy
With the accursed holiness that pursues
Descendants for many generations.

But the lament of Antigone
Searching for her brother
Is indeed beyond the power
Of endurance. And the heart
Is a stone in which is enclosed,
Like an insect, the dark love
Of a most unhappy land.

I did not want to love so.
That was not my design.

I did not want to pity so.
That was not my design.
My pen is lighter
Than a hummingbird's feather. This burden
Is too much for it to bear.

"You swore never to touch / The deep wounds of
your nation": Miłosz was aware of the strain of
martyrology in Poland's self-image—not entirely
unfounded, given its history of partitions, Siberian exile, and violent Russian domination—as
well as a tendency to Romantic heroism, which
at the beginning of the war led the Polish cavalry
to ride out against German tanks to the accom-
paniment of Chopin's "Heroic" polonaise being
broadcast on Polish radio. He was temperamentally averse to such transports of patriotism, but
in the poem, restrained by the frame of form, are
the anguish and sorrow he did not allow himself
in most of his prose writings about the war. Why
didn't he? Was it for fear of the nagging "insect" getting out of its enclosure and dissolving the stony heart's protective containment?
Of being overwhelmed by emotions from which
no detachment was possible? ("The lament of
Antigone": I think of my father, at the war's end,
having to bury two of his brothers himself, in
a grassy field on the outskirts of his shtetl; the

burden of such knowledge is indeed not easily bearable.) The implications of the poem's powerful metaphors are not reducible to literal explanations, but the force of feeling that drove Miłosz's poetry—and which is so evident here—surely exacted its price in the pain of pity and love as well as in scorn and rage.

Eventually, in a kind of coda to his autobiographical account of the wartime years, Miłosz gives full vent to the depth and violence of his passions, and his sense that the extent of both the Polish and the Jewish tragedy was too enormous for ordinary sympathy or sadness. "Had I been given the chance," he writes, "perhaps I would have blown the country to bits, so that mothers would no longer cry over their seventeen-year-old sons and daughters who died on the barricades, so that the grass would no longer grow over the ashes of Treblinka and Maidanek and Auschwitz, so that the notes of a harmonica played under a gnarled pine tree would no longer float over the nightmarish pits and dunes on the city outskirts. Because there is a kind of pity that is unbearable. And so one blows it all up, at least in one's mind; that is, one is possessed by a single desire: not to look."

If one wants to understand the sources of Miłosz's detachment from the war's terrible events, perhaps one should look for them, not in indifference, but in an intensity of feelings too deep for sorrow—or even tragic lament.

◈ For anyone who lived through the cataclysm of World War II, there would always be "before" and "after." So it was for Miłosz, but his trajectory in the early postwar years continued to be dauntingly complicated, in its circumstances and geographic movements as well as in the motions of his mind. In 1945 he wrote several emotionally charged responses to the tragedy, including one of his best-known poems, "Dedication":

> You whom I could not save
> Listen to me.
> Try to understand this simple speech as I
>   would be ashamed of another.
> I swear, there is in me no wizardry of words.
> I speak to you with silence like a cloud or a
>   tree. . . .
>
> What is poetry which does not save
> Nations or people?
> A connivance with official lies,
> A song of drunkards whose throats will be
>   cut in a moment,
> Readings for sophomore girls.
> That I wanted good poetry without
>   knowing it,

That I discovered, late, its salutary aim,
In this and only this I find salvation.

The poem is a plea for reprieve from the guilt of survival, and it sounds notes that would inform a series of politically—and morally—intricate decisions Miłosz made after the war, which led to dramatic changes in his situation. To go along with the new, Soviet-sponsored government or not: that was the dilemma for all postwar intellectuals in Poland. Many did, and so, initially, did Miłosz, refusing to go as far as signing up for the Communist Party—he was never a "card-carrying Communist"—but accepting the post of cultural attaché at the Polish embassy in Washington, DC. For the party, whose leadership realized the value of recruiting a liberal, well-known writer and intellectual, he was a useful acquisition. On his end, Miłosz thought that his diplomatic position would enable him to continue writing poetry more freely than he could under the censorious eye of the regime in Poland: a consideration that trumped many others, leading to the choice he thought would allow him to pursue his life's first purpose and task.

Miłosz's postwar years in America were his first experience of a kind of exile—or, at least, of being an alien abroad. (He notes, with his usual punctiliousness, that the letters "DP" on his car's license plate did not denote a "Displaced Person" but the status of "Diplomatic Personnel.") In his recollections of that time, he dismisses Washington, with its political intrigues and vast bureaucratic web, with a stroke of a pen ("an impersonal machine, a pure abstraction"), but he notes with pleasure the surprising discovery of great expanses of wild nature in America—a country he imagined from afar as being entirely covered by industrial and urban landscapes. He was drawn particularly to the wilderness of the northern states, which reminded him of the forests and wilderness of his childhood. "I plunged into books on American flora and fauna, made diplomatic contacts with porcupines and beavers in the forests of Pennsylvania," he writes, allowing himself passages of playful charm.

The nature of human culture, however, was a different matter—and the essence of the problem, in that first transplantation, was the American sense of time. "My circumstances brought about an acute recurrence of my old sickness," he writes, "which I may have suffered from even in high school. . . . It consists of a disturbance in one's perception of time. The sick man constantly sees time as an hourglass through which states, systems, and civilizations trickle like sand; his immediate surroundings lose the force of reality . . . in other words, being is unreal, only movement is real."

Miłosz's acute awareness of time's passage was undoubtedly exacerbated by the war and all its personal and collective losses. "I could not stop my mind from coursing through the ages like a projectile," he writes, whereas Americans, in his view, suffered—without knowing it—from the opposite malady: "A loss of the sense of history and, therefore, of a sense of the tragic, which is only born of historical experience." America, of course, was the land of the future: of constant progress, the promise of the promised land, of the American Dream. But when he first glimpsed New York on arrival in America, he did not throb with a sense of optimistic expectation as so many immigrants did. Instead, he was angry: how did the city have the impudence to show off its glamorous skyscrapers as if nothing had happened?

Miłosz therefore observed America as if he were "an anthropologist," a mode of perception that, to my mind, is a fundamental aspect of the emigrant and the exilic mind. From the often discomfiting position between cultures, you can see certain basic assumptions that remain invisible to those who are embedded within them. In that early transplantation, Miłosz was struck by a particular mode of competitive individualism in America, and an aggressiveness "channeled into the struggle for money," which, however, led not only to achieving self-enrichment (at least for a select few) but to "an inner sterility." He also spoke about Americans' prevailing conviction that their country was the norm, to which the rest of humanity should aspire.

These were aspects of what was then still called "the American character," which struck me, almost verbatim, in the first stages of my own emigration to America—and which made the felt experience of living there, even at my younger (and putatively more adaptable) age, one of odd and hardly admissible estrangement. In another vein, I wonder if it was pure coincidence that some decades later I wrote a book called *Human Time*. My preoccupation with this subject did not emerge from a *longue durée* understanding of history—that knowledge which for Miłosz was almost his sixth sense—but it was fed by my experience of different cultures and their very different modalities of lived time. Postwar Poland was all past; America all future. But the great power's much-vaunted optimism did not seem to make for a sense of individual enjoyment, or capacity to take pleasure in lived experience, in the moment; on the contrary, attitudes to the passage of time were fraught with anxiety. Time was money, after all, and the aim was not to waste a moment or droplet of it in useless activities or idle enjoyment. This was in great contrast to postwar Poland, where there were no great careers or fortunes to be made; where conversations around the kitchen table could go on late into the night; where moments of pensive contemplation—or simply experiencing a moment fully—were highly valued. Cultural differences go deep, and it is one of the discoveries of the "anthropological" emigrant perspective that they extend to every aspect of experience, including the seemingly most abstract coordinates within which we live—the dimensions of space and time. But, to continue for a moment in a confessional vein, if I wanted to write about time, that was also because I was time-obsessed since childhood; a condition fueled, I think, by the historical moment and place into which I was born—by the sense, so clearly felt by many children growing up then, that life was provisional and death ubiquitous and omnipresent. This was not, of course, comparable to Miłosz's actual experience of catastrophe, but I wonder if the juxtaposition of recent, all-encompassing destruction with hollow American optimism might have made for that "acute recurrence" of his "sickness" and his exacerbated awareness that everything solid can all too easily melt into air.

Miłosz's diplomatic post at the Polish embassy in Washington did indeed enable him to write as he wanted, outside his rather undemanding work hours, but he was never comfortable in his role, performing a bureaucratic job even as his contempt for bureaucracy remained unabated. Moreover, he felt the distrust of his colleagues, who suspected, rightly, that by the lights of the regnant regime, he was not quite politically correct. Nor did he particularly relish the naïve fascination of the embassy's liberal guests, who felt all too excited at meeting a real "red."

In 1946 he wrote a long poem filled with a sense of unusually bitter irony, called "Child of Europe." Here are a few segments from what is a sardonic picture of a compromised postwar Europe and also, perhaps, a confession of his own, uneasy bad faith:

> We, who taste of exotic dishes,
> And enjoy fully the delights of love,
> Are better than those who were buried. . . .
>
> Having the choice of our own death and that
>   of a friend,
> We chose his, coldly thinking: let it be done
>   quickly. . . .
>
> Treasure your legacy of skills, child of
>   Europe

Inheritor of Gothic cathedrals, of baroque
   churches,
Of synagogues filled with the wailing of a
   wronged people,
Successor of Descartes, Spinoza, inheritor
   of the word "honor,"
Posthumous child of Leonidas,
Treasure the skills acquired in the hour of
   terror.

You have a clever mind which sees
   instantly
The good and bad of any situation.
You have an elegant, skeptical mind which
   enjoys pleasures
Quite unknown to primitive races. . . .

There can be no question of force triumphant.
We live in the age of victorious justice. . . .

He who has power, has it by historical logic.
Respectfully bow to that logic.

The part of "Europe" Miłosz is referring to most
immediately is, of course, postwar Poland—and
the poem's barbed ironies are directed at the hy-
pocrisies and sophistries required of those who,
by whatever means, survived mass death and
now serve the new regime. Given the "we" of the
poem, this implicitly, and bitterly, includes himself. But Poland was also the country at the cen-

ter of the war's vortex, which revealed the failure of Europe as a whole: the failure, despite its legacy of high civilization, to defend its allies and its values; to rescue one half of the continent from takeover by a ruthless dictatorship; to prevent the Iron Curtain from descending. Europe, with its "elegant, skeptical mind" was willing to use its cleverness, and its sophistries, to justify its betrayals and to usher in the age—in the poem's acidly ironic phrase—of "victorious justice."

Eventually, the ironies and the necessity of bad faith inherent in his own position became too disturbing, and in the early 1950s Miłosz decided to abandon his U.S. diplomatic post and to defect to France. The choices preceding this difficult step were anguished. In 1949 Miłosz made a visit to Poland and was appalled by the economic ravages the Soviet-sponsored regime had inflicted on the country, the ubiquitous hatred of the new authorities he felt everywhere, the dread and hatred of its representatives (which, he could sense, was directed at him as well), and the sacrifice of integrity exacted from those who, in serving the New Order, had to submit to its humiliations. Miłosz did not want to see fear in people's eyes as they talked to him, and he could not silence that moral faculty which assured him that what was happening in his native country was deeply wrong. In the end, he said later, what drove him into exile were not ideological considerations but "a revolt of the stomach."

Possibly, also, the ironies of his poetry became too much of a reproach to himself as well as to others. In the poem "You Who Wronged," dated Washington, 1950, he writes:

You who have wronged a simple man . . .

. . . Do not feel safe. The poet remembers.
You can kill one, but another is born.
The words are written down, the deed, the
    date.

Nevertheless, the decision to defect continued to be highly fraught, and in his effort to resolve the conflict, he even went so far as to consult Albert Einstein about his dilemma. With his respect for science, it is no wonder that Miłosz hoped the sage would offer answers underpinned by incontrovertible reasons—and Reason. But if that was what he wanted, he was disappointed. Einstein simply told him he should "stick to his own country," but the great scientist's understanding of what that country had become was, to Miłosz's mind, insufficient and proceeded from a very different, "humanist" era. Perhaps this was unfair. Einstein surely cannot be seen as a naïve humanist, but neither could he be expected to enter fully into the dilemmas of a Polish poet-diplomat. Nor could Einstein have predicted that in America's increasingly repressive, McCarthyite atmosphere, Miłosz soon after came to be perceived, in a twist of very unpoetic irony, as a Communist sympathizer, and barred from reentering the United States as an immigrant.

Before that, however, as his disloyalty became clear, he was recalled from his diplomatic post to Poland, where his passport was confiscated. His wife, Janina, who was pregnant with their second child, remained in the United States, and according to the recollections of his friends, the uncertainty of the situation threw Miłosz into great turmoil and depression. Luckily, Miłosz's prewar connections, which now extended to people in influential positions, still held; and after a clandestine, high-level intervention from one of his friends, the new authorities finally provided him with a passport and a diplomatic position in France. Indeed, he used the passport to travel to France, but when he arrived there, instead of taking up his position, he asked for asylum—which was granted. With this step, as he notes, he became a refugee—a status very different from that of an immigrant or even an exile. Initially, he went into hiding, for fear of the long reach of Communist authorities, but whatever the hardships of his situation, he was relieved to be, once again, in Paris.

Physically, the city remained almost magically unchanged; a contrast with ruined Warsaw, which accounted for his initial amazement, and which was an objective correlative for the stark differences in the two countries' recent history. But the historical chasm also meant that between his first, student stay in Paris and his new sojourn, Miłosz's perceptions of France changed considerably—as did his sense of what it meant to be from the Other Europe. This time, he was not awed by the putative superiority of French culture; he knew that despite its love of freedom, France had failed to come to Poland's aid during the war, that its great culture did not save it from widespread collaboration with the Nazi regime or from viciously persecuting and deporting French Jews, beyond the demands of its German overseers.

Miłosz's situation in France held its own share of tangled postwar ironies. "I was trying to make the best of my fall in Paris," he writes, "for the lot of a refugee is such a fall." The truth was that he was not only separated from his wife and two children, but he had no way of making a living, and it did not help that he was caught in an entirely new web of political misunderstandings. French intellectual life in those years was dominated by Sartre and his circle, most of whom prided themselves on their pro-Communist sympathies, and Miłosz, in alluding to this in his recollections, allows himself a rare instance of sarcastic resentment. "A writer who fled from a country where Tomorrow was being born (if the system is bad, then it is good enough for Eastern barbarians) was guilty of *a social blunder*." His status in Parisian society wavered between that "of a pickpocket and of a swindler"—although in his case, one prominent enough to be regularly attacked by what he called "the Stalinist press." But this time, rather than feeling the inferiority of coming from that other, putatively less civilized part of Europe, he felt it was the *bien pensants* of the French left who were arrested in the past and guilty of that great Sartrean sin—bad faith. Indeed, Sartre's and De Beauvoir's support of the Soviet-sponsored regimes, their visits to Poland, and their admiration for China during the Cultural Revolution showed a degree either of naïveté or hypocrisy that were quite stunning. Interestingly, one of Miłosz's few supporters among the French intelligentsia was Albert Camus. Was that partly because he came from a colonized country himself? Camus was an anti-Communist who eventually broke with Sartre, but the quiet fury of his best-known protagonist—Meursault, in *The Stranger*—suggests he would have understood Miłosz's outsider position and his scorn.

When I interviewed Miłosz in his Berkeley home in 1981, I was particularly struck by his account of his French years. Although in his writing he eventually found a way to reconcile himself to France and Europe, what I felt in his recollections of that period was a still fresh energy of anger. He talked about being a pariah among the intelligentsia; about being taken for a right-wing anti-Communist, when this description hardly fit the case; about being intellectually ostracized; about not being able to get published. He told me that the idea of writing his novel, *The Seizure of Power*, came out of these circumstances. He decided to write it very quickly (with the help, as I remember, of someone who could supervise his French), in order to submit it for the Prix Européen—on the gamble that it might win and bring in some much-needed income. It did win, and as Miłosz told me this, his very thick eyebrows went up and down, and his tone betrayed just a hint of satirical satisfaction.

Indeed, given the literary vanguard's rejection of Miłosz's opinions and writing from that period, he may well have felt that he pulled off something of a very elaborate ruse in winning the prize—since the novel's hurly-burly plot and large cast of characters clearly reflect a range of ideas and attitudes that the Parisian elites of the time found so unpalatable. Perhaps the jury wasn't of their number. But a novel can also dramatize ambivalences and ambiguities without "irritable reaching" after certainties or declaring clear-cut ideological positions, in ways that more direct forms of expression—or, for that matter, Miłosz's actions—could not. And *The Seizure of Power* is really a novel about both external and internal chaos. It contains scenes of the Soviet army marching into Poland, the novel's main protagonist among them; depictions of the Warsaw Uprising's last, awful moments, with people dying among the rubble of bombed and gutted buildings; desperate escapes through sewers (an aspect of the uprising immortalized in Andrzej Wajda's film *Canal*); and the installation of the new, Soviet order, with its naïve foot soldiers and ruthless leaders. There is a moving scene of two strangers caught in a building, standing in the line of fire, in what may be the last moments of their lives, making love to each other in silent, complete understanding. (Such an episode was described in Jan Kott's much later memoir, *Still Alive*, and one can imagine other instances of "love among the ruins" in these end-of-the-world circumstances.)

Mostly, however, *The Seizure of Power* is a novel of conversations and internal dialogues, which dramatize both the external conflicts among the new rulers and the newly ruled—and the inner self-divisions of various characters, as they try to figure out whether and how to adjust to the new order. The main characters on the vanquished (i.e., Polish) side belong to the cultured and intellectual classes, and in the novel, they are fully conscious of the implications of their choices. To cooperate with the new authorities—or not? And if they decide not to be co-opted—then what? The potential consequences might have included the loss of social position, of university posts, of the chance to make a living. Several of the novel's characters are Jewish and have lost relatives in concentration camps or the Warsaw ghetto; mostly, they are willing to go along with the Soviet-installed order—and, sometimes, to play important roles in it. At least the Soviets did not have the infernal idea of exterminating an entire people—and declared themselves to be ethnically blind. (In actuality, as Miłosz knew, a large proportion of the horribly reduced Jewish population that remained in Poland after the war—about 300,000 out of three million—survived the horror in the Soviet Union, and for understandable reasons, the proportion of Jews in Poland's postwar Communist Party was high, leading to new tensions and new versions of anti-Semitism.) In *Seizure*, there are other nuances among the newly powerful Communists. Some of them are as educated and conscious of the "dialectic of history" as their opponents and are willing to turn a blind eye to "ideological impurities" if a person can play a useful role—no matter how well everyone understands that they are playacting. Catholics who sign up to the party can be particularly useful, given the Polish population's attachment to the faith.

All this reflected the new, bitterly confusing realities. But the main dilemma in the novel belongs to its Miłosz-like protagonist, Peter Kwinto: to stay—or to defect? To stay, in the novel as in life, would mean writing poetry to order, as some of Miłosz's wartime friends were already doing; it would require the protagonist to betray himself in various ways and to become a figure of hatred among ordinary people for whom he feels the strongest affinity. But to leave—does that mean not accepting reality? Kwinto hates what the old Poland, with its nationalism and right-leaning conservatism, stood for; at least the new order is new. Does it represent the dialectical movement of history, which has to be accepted—and is escaping from it tantamount to evading something inevitable? In the end he defects, flying to France and the no-longer-mythical West.

In nonfictional form, Miłosz tackled similar themes in *The Captive Mind*—a brilliant analysis, written in the early 1950s, of the situation of writers and intellectuals in the Soviet sphere, with which he achieved, for the first time, international recognition. This had its measure of irony, not only because *The Captive Mind* is a difficult book, but because—as Miłosz makes perfectly clear in a foreword to the 1981 English-language edition—it was intended not only as a decoding of the compromises and contorted maneuvers performed by Polish intellectuals held in the vice of a totalitarian system but as a critique of the French intelligentsia, who "placed their hopes on a new world in the East, ruled by a leader of incomparable wisdom and virtue, Stalin." The note of sharp sarcasm suggests that the anger I heard in his voice when he talked about his French period was indeed deep and long-lasting. But so was the larger relevance of his subject, which, he says in his introduction, is "the vulnerability of the twentieth-century mind to seduction by socio-political doctrines and its readiness to accept totalitarian terror for the sake of a hypothetical future." This is something he alludes to in his memoir, his essays, and his poems; the underlying reason for such susceptibility, he implies again and again, is the loss of religion and other explanatory systems of morality and meaning, and their replacement by the "New Faith"—that is, the theory of dialectical materialism, or "Diamat." For abstracting intellectuals suffering from "fear of sterility," Diamat, with its rejection of the bourgeoisie and its ideal of creating a New Man, provided, in his view, an ostensible vision of purpose and progress. The thinly disguised Polish writers and intellectuals whom Miłosz portrays in *The Captive Mind* (and most of whom he knew personally) did not conform to the totalitarian rules of artistic production out of sheer submission. Sometimes they did so in the spirit of pure hypocrisy and bad faith, but more often they played complicated games with the system—and above all, with their own minds—to persuade themselves that they actually believed in what they were doing: that the New Faith stood for progress and the inevitable direction of History.

But for those who couldn't deceive themselves completely, the mind games often had dark consequences. Perhaps the most tragic chapter in *Captive Mind* is the portrait of Beta, a pseudonym for Tadeusz Borowski, who later became known to Western readers for his collection of short stories titled, with terrifying irony, *This Way for the Gas, Ladies and Gentlemen*. Miłosz knew Borowski in Warsaw during the war, when he was a natural rebel and a highly promising, haughty, and shy young poet. He was captured by the Germans and sent to Auschwitz—one of the numerous non-Jewish Poles whose great privilege in the camps was that they were not slated for immediate extermination. The stories in Borowski's book are very different in style and tone from Primo Levi's *If This Is a Man*, but they are similar in their understanding that the inhuman conditions of the camps dehumanized not only the Nazi overseers but the inmates as well. Throughout the stories, examples of the treatment that the more "advantaged" prisoners meted out to the weaker are nearly unbearable to read—especially since Borowski implicates himself as one of the tormentors. But this, as Miłosz points out, is an expression of a strong moral sense rather than its deficiency. Borowski understands the distinction between what, in such circumstances, can rightfully be called good and evil, and he ruthlessly levels judgment at himself as well as others. After the war, the Auschwitz stories were published in Poland, and Borowski, as a talented author of powerfully anti-Nazi writing who could be useful to the regime, was given good journalistic jobs. These, however, required him to write sheer propaganda. This he did apparently with a will—until 1951, when he committed suicide at the age of twenty-eight by turning on the gas in his apartment. The link between cause and effect wasn't entirely clear, but for Miłosz, the loss of integrity and self-betrayal that Borowski—

after enduring horrors—exacted from himself in order to be a government hack was at least a contributing cause of his death.

The other portraits in *Captive Mind* are less tragic, but they all show talented writers who compromised their art and themselves, sometimes out of desire for importance and position in the new order, but just as often so as not to be left out of that great and abstract desideratum—the progress of History. Moreover, if they wrote in a sufficiently correct mode, they were guaranteed a large readership, which consisted not only of the elites but of the masses. "Correct" books were distributed by publishing houses in officially mandated, quite large numbers, and as Miłosz notes, what writer, anywhere, could resist that? Nevertheless, the deceptions and self-deceptions required by the tyranny of Communist political correctness exacted their toll. The thinly disguised writers who are the protagonists of *Captive Mind* descended into alcoholism and despair, producing shamelessly sloganeering kitsch. The loss of individual self-respect could not be measured in simple ways, but it was augmented by a larger loss to Polish literature, which, as Miłosz notes, became in this period mostly unreadable.

Miłosz was saved from self-betrayal by his devotion—not to any collective faith, old or new, but to his calling, which was poetry—and by his absolute refusal to compromise the integrity and seriousness of his art. Finding forms for poetry equal to the gravity of the times was his main goal even during the terrible years of the war, and his willingness to serve the Polish government for a while was driven by his need to continue writing in his native tongue.

But at the end of *Captive Mind* he gives another reason for his choices and his mode of resistance by invoking a seemingly small, trivial incident. At the beginning of the war, he found himself in the Soviet Union at a train station full of "sleeping beggars," while, over their bodies, "loudspeakers shouted propaganda slogans." It was a portent of things to come. In the midst of the melee, he saw a peasant family, which happened to be whispering in Polish, as the parents were feeding their children. "The gesture of a hand pouring tea," he says, "the careful, delicate handing of the cup to the child . . . their isolation, their privacy in the midst of the crowd— that is what moved me." It is a poignantly moving passage for the reader as well. As always, it is the ordinary, the simple human gesture that speaks to Miłosz of what we are, and that truth of the human condition which he tries again and again to discover and describe—and not to betray.

But as Miłosz, with his moral punctiliousness, was all too aware, for a while he might well have been accused of bad faith himself. In the later foreword to the English-language edition of *The Captive Mind*, he feels compelled to give yet another reason for remaining associated with the Polish government for as long as he did (although he was the first high-level figure to defect from Poland): "It was to avoid exile . . . the worst of all misfortunes." It is hard to know if the reasoning was partly retrospective; exile, after all, was a fruitful condition for quite a few writers, and in some ways for Miłosz as well. But the first, Parisian phase of his exiled life was indeed difficult in the extreme. In addition to being ejected from his native tongue, which, he feared, would bring "sterility and inaction," he was separated from his wife and two sons, one of whom was born without his being present. Moreover, for someone who had thought, understood—experienced—so much, the ostracism he met with in Paris must have been bitter; and I confess that, even in long retrospect, I occasionally feel fruitlessly angry on his behalf and annoyed by the continuing intellectual idealization of Sartre—a thinker who wrote some of the key works of the twentieth century but whose sense of moral superiority in relation to Miłosz and other exiles from the Soviet sphere was entirely unwarranted. For Sartre and his faithful followers, their pro-Soviet sympathies and their fascination with Chinese communism were a form of ideological posturing without costs or consequences. For Miłosz, his impossible choices—made on deeply considered grounds— had life-changing repercussions. Perhaps it was the crucial difference between Sartre and Miłosz that Sartre's pro-Communist positions emerged from ideas and their transposition into ideology, while Miłosz's choices were propelled by head-on collisions with hard, consequence-bearing realities.

(I should say that if I was particularly interested in Miłosz's account of his Parisian years, that was partly because it threw a new light on some of the conflicts and misunderstandings I felt during the long 1960s, when I was a graduate student at Harvard—for all that I was grateful to be received at that institution so soon after my own arrival on American shores. There were good reasons for my fellow students' radical rebellions: the Vietnam War had been unfolding in all its horror, and its awful images were reaching Americans—for the first time in the history of wars—on television. I was not a politically formed creature, but I felt I naturally belonged "on the left"—if only because of the distinctly underprivileged and socially marginal position my family occupied after emigration, and, for that matter, before that as well. But in the endless conversations in the student cafeteria, or as I listened to the pronouncements of student protesters, I often felt inarticulate anger rising in my throat. Immigrant rage, I came to call it, and I felt its rise at my fellow students' entirely uninformed pro-Soviet sympathies; at their fervent admiration for China's Cultural Revolution; at the naïve idealization of "the workers," who would have much rather fought my Harvard friends down to the ground than launched their hoped-for revolution. Most of all, I felt, when I dared express my opinions, those fellow students' patronizing scorn. My views simply didn't count—and neither did the country or the part of Europe from which I derived. There was a fundamental and very credulous misunderstanding in all this that continued "on the left" for quite a long time. Soviet-sponsored communism was seen as a radically progressive philosophy rather than what it actually was: an exceptionally repressive, reactionary ideology and form of governance. My fellow students' admiration for the Soviet Union was also my initiation into the phenomenon that Miłosz analyzed so incisively: the strange power of ideology to influence our perceptions of reality and, in a postreligious age, its almost religious force.)

Miłosz, of course, became acquainted with such phenomena well before the cool sixties. To add to the discomforts of his French exile, even as he was ostracized by the French left, he was also shunned by prewar, mostly conservative Polish émigrés, who suspected him of Communist sympathies. It was not an enviable position. Fortunately, however, he found a literary and intellectual home—if not a sufficient source of income—in a wonderful émigré institution called the Literary Institute, located in the Parisian suburb of Maisons-Laffitte, where it published a magazine called *Kultura*. During the Cold War decades, *Kultura*'s distinguished publications were largely responsible for keeping dissident Polish culture alive. With the aid of underground networks, *Kultura* published exiled or censored Polish writers, most of whom were then largely unknown outside Poland, but some of whose names have since entered the world's literary canon. The cheeky, highly experimental writer Witold Gombrowicz, then living in Argentinian exile; the future Nobelist Wisława Szymborska; and the philosopher Leszek Kołakowski—eventually Oxford-based—were among them. Non-Polish writers such as André Malraux, Albert Camus, E. M. Cioran, and T. S. Eliot also appeared in its pages.

In a lovely essay about one of the Literary Institute's founders, Zygmunt Hertz, Miłosz describes a collective (he's reluctant to call it a "commune") in which everyone lived together, cooked together, and worked on writing, editing, printing, and distributing books together. Miłosz describes it as an "insane undertaking," which had to perpetually struggle to survive, and which was, in the reigning political climate of the time, isolated from French intellectual life. This provokes Miłosz to an unusually overt expression of scorn, which he was perhaps reluctant to give vent to quite so directly on his own behalf. "The West European, or at least Parisian, spirit," he writes, "was wallowing in existential melancholy because of its lost chance, that is, because the western part of the continent had been liberated by the wrong, read 'capitalist,' army. The few people who stammered out that maybe this was actually for the good were condemned as American agents, socially ostracized, and also dragged into the courts."

Poland, even before the terrible twentieth century, had a long history of emigration—particularly to France, and *Kultura* had distinguished precursors in a group of nineteenth-century exiles from Russian domination who included, among others, Frédéric Chopin and the great poet Adam Mickiewicz, the Polish bard, with whom Miłosz felt considerable affinity, and to whom he is sometimes compared. Those earlier émigrés, Miłosz notes, were welcomed to France because they were fleeing from Russian oppression and were seen as "defenders of freedom." Not so the defectors from the Communist utopia.

But the fascinating group of people gathered at Maisons-Laffitte, where *Kultura* resided for most of its duration, had each other, and they had true solidarity. Some of this spirit can be glimpsed in Miłosz's essay on Hertz, who provided, not without considerable personal risk, the funding that kept Maisons-Laffitte going. The essay is a tribute to a friend, and to someone who had a talent for friendship. It is also, in Miłosz's oeuvre, an unusually intimate portrait of someone he admired, to whom he could talk about all his doubts and troubles, with whom he sometimes disagreed, and who, in turn, could say anything to him. "Czesiu," Hertz would say (using the diminutive of Miłosz's name), "don't talk, you'll say something stupid. Write." Or "write for people," he would also say, meaning that Miłosz's poetry should be more accessible, but there, Miłosz could not oblige. His poetic principles trumped all other considerations.

One poem written for particular people in 1959, titled "What Once Was Great," is dedicated "To A. and O. Wat"—that is, Aleksander and Ola Wat, a modernist poet and his wife who had their own, separate odysseys during the war, with Aleksander enduring a stint in the infamous Lubyanka prison, and Ola suffering extreme hardships in the far-flung regions of the Soviet empire:

> What once was great, now appeared small.
> Kingdoms were fading like snow-covered
> bronze.
>
> What once could smite, now smites no
> more.
> Celestial earths roll on and shine.
>
> Stretched on the grass by the bank of a
> river,
> As long, long ago, I launch my boats of bark.

Later, Miłosz did a series of interviews with Aleksander, in the hope of distracting him from the state of chronic pain his friend suffered after his experiences, which were published in one of the great memoirs of the time, called *My Century*.

I don't think I'm idealizing when I say that a sort of talent, a predilection for friendship runs deep in Polish culture. Friendship was the fuel of the youthful groups to which Miłosz belonged, with their nicknames and disputes, their shared adventures and misadventures. And I was lucky enough to get to know another group of emigrants, many of whom left Poland in 1968, when the turns of the political wheel turned on university students and Jewish members of the Communist Party, and when a considerable part of the Jewish intelligentsia left for Israel, the United States, Italy, and elsewhere. The group I came to know in New York in the 1970s was a unique political phenomenon: it consisted mostly of dissidents who came from families of leading Communists. "Good Communists," for the most part—that is, people who joined the party out of initial idealism, no matter how disabused they may have become later. The parents often disagreed with their rebellious children but did not want to interfere with their political views or activities; perhaps they recognized in the younger generation a repetition of their own idealism— however different its expression.

Many of my friends knew one another from childhood, and, like Miłosz's early travel companions (nicknamed Robespierre and Elephant), they had fond nicknames and diminutives for each other. (Polish has diminutives for almost all first names, and objects, a form of intimacy embedded in the language.) As I learned more about my transplanted friends, I found out that many of them grew up in the same, relatively privileged neighborhood of Warsaw, attended the same schools, and spent various periods of time in prison. Once abroad, they retained their ties across various borders, as well as with friends who remained in Poland, and later formed the core of Solidarity's intellectual wing. At some point, I started referring to them as members of "PS1, Warsaw" (after New York's system of numbering public schools in this manner), and, eventually, I was informally accepted as an honorary member of that group. I continue to be rather proud of the title.

At Maisons-Laffitte, friendships extended to the delicate area of creativity, and I wonder if in his injunction to Miłosz, Hertz might have been thinking of *A Treatise on Poetry*—the extremely complex, book-length poem Miłosz was writing in 1955–56. The *Treatise* was initially published by *Kultura*, whose readership was highly cultivated but very small, and Miłosz thought it would never be translated into English. He was wrong about that—it was published by Ecco Press in 2001—that is, after his Nobel and accession to worldwide fame. But at the time he was composing this complex, idiosyncratic, and impassioned work, he may have been doing it really for its own sake, and perhaps as a kind of reckoning. It is yet another effort to explain something about his native realm—this time, through a condensed history of Polish poetry and its vicissitudes during the twentieth century. The short section called "Preface" is a kind of aesthetic manifesto:

> First, plain speech in the mother tongue.
> Hearing it, you should be able to see
> Apple trees, a river, the bend of a road,
> As if in a flash of summer lightning.
>
> And it should contain more than images.
> It has been lured by singsong,
> A daydream, melody. Defenseless,
> It was bypassed by the sharp, dry world.
>
> You often ask yourself why you feel shame
> Whenever you look through a book of poetry.
> As if the author, for reasons unclear to you,
> Addressed the worse side of your nature,
> Pushing aside thought, cheating thought. . . .
>
> And our regret has remained unconfessed.
> Novels and essays serve but will not last.
> One clear stanza can take more weight
> Than a whole wagon of elaborate prose.

The *Treatise* certainly delivers confrontation with the "sharp, dry world." In addition to sixty pages of poetry, it contains another sixty of explanatory notes—much needed, especially for English-language readers. Its four sections progress from Kraków in the early twentieth century, when the city was still part of the Austro-Hungarian empire, to "The Capital," about Warsaw in the interwar period, to "The Spirit of History" subtitled Warsaw, 1939–1945, and—startlingly—a final section called "Natura," situated in Pennsylvania, 1948–49. The first three sections are full of exact and vivid detail evoking the mood of time and place. ("This is our beginning / useless to recall a distant golden age / We have to accept and take as our own / The moustache with pomade, the bowler hat acock.") They contain condensed, vivid vignettes of Polish poets, many of whom Miłosz knew well, and some of whom were lost during the war. There are evocations of their personalities and their aesthetic views but also, importantly, an analysis of their rare successes, and their more frequent failures in grappling with the actualities of history and politics. ("Gałczyński wanted to fall on his knees. / His story contains an elemental truth, namely that a poet without a community / Rustles in the wind like dry grass in December . . . / Let it be stated here clearly: the Party / Descends directly from the fascist Right.") Some parts of the *Treatise* allude to the same material as *The Captive Mind*, and most of this extensive, difficult work reads like a philosophical disquisition in verse. Plato would not have had reason to throw this poet out of his Republic.

The poem's last section, "Natura," can be read as a coda and counterpoint to the more historical and more turbulent sections. Within this sequence, the poet sits in a boat at night, waiting for a beaver to appear—and remembering other encounters with nature in eidetic detail. In his writings, Miłosz often cautions against using nature for symbolic purposes or attributing to it human meanings, but even during his most difficult French years, it was in nature that he found the greatest succor. Without it, he implies, he might have fallen into depression (or, as he calls it, in a religiously tinged formulation, "*delectatio morosa*"). Perhaps, then, the last section of the *Treatise* is his attempt to come to terms with— or to overcome—the disillusionment that permeates the poem's previous sections. Affirmation, for Miłosz, was a need and a moral imperative; nature, here, is succor and compensation for the arid actualities of a very imperfect world.

Of course, lucky is the lover of beauty who comes to live in France, and quite a few poems written from Montgeron (a semirural suburb of Paris where Miłosz lived during most of his

French years) are evocations of landscapes and living creatures, often combining very exact observations with a sense of fundamental amazement at the very facts of being, rather than its opposite, and contemplating the nature of nature itself—as in "Ode to a Bird":

O composite,

O unconscious,

Holding your feathery palms behind you,
Propped on your gray lizard legs,
On cybernetic gloves
That grasp at whatever they touch.

O incommensurate.
Larger than the precipice
In a lily-of-the-valley . . .

More vast than a galleried night
With the headlights of an ant—
And a galaxy in its body
Indeed, equal to any.

Nature, for Miłosz, contains its own immense microcosms. But the terrain of France, aside from its natural beauty, was imbricated with history, as the American landscapes Miłosz had briefly visited were not, and this, for him, was a crucial difference. For generations of francophile Poles—and indeed, for many others—France, even in the postwar period, stood for all that was desirable about Europe: for pleasure-loving urban life and grandeur of cathedrals, for elegance and refined cuisine, for civilization itself. Miłosz's urge for wonder and affirmation—his pansexuality—was strong, and despite his anger at Sartre & Co., despite his contempt for French behavior during the war, he refound, in his wanderings through that country, his affinity for "Europe herself" and acknowledged, once again, that "in spite of my refusal to accept her split and her sickliness, Europe, after all, was home to me."

🎴 Europe was home, but it was a home Miłosz eventually had to leave. This was not directly because of the ideological and intellectual discomforts he felt in France but for simpler reasons, of the kind that had driven great numbers of people to migrate to America before. Quite simply, in France, Miłosz could not make a living or, once he was reunited with his wife and two sons, support his family. So when in 1960 he received an offer of a teaching position in the Slavic Department at Berkeley, he accepted— although he had never taught before, was not in possession of a PhD, and had no ambitions for an academic career. The very fact of the offer was a telling contrast to the attitudes he encountered in

France, and, whatever reservations he might have had about American culture, Miłosz was grateful to his new country for welcoming him, as it had welcomed so many others. As he noted, America was a country of exiles; in its setting, his was not an exceptional condition. That meant, among other things, that if, in France, he often felt misunderstood, in America, for much of his period there, he was simply unnoticed. He was a professor in the Slavic department, some of whose courses attracted substantial numbers of students, but who, in other ways—as a writer and, especially, a poet—remained unknown even to most of his colleagues.

At the same time, America—especially its far western, Californian coast—posed a challenge to his powers of perception and understanding. It was, in every sense of the word, very far from Europe, and much of his writing from that time is an attempt to decode that distance and understand the deeply unfamiliar place where he so unexpectedly found himself. This is especially true of the essays written during his American decades. In the poems, his imagination turns more often to the increasingly remote past—and to memorialization.

These are the two-pronged aspects of the exilic imagination, and when, from my own emigrant position in the United States, I turned to

Miłosz's writings from that period—especially the interconnected essays in *Visions from San Francisco Bay*—I felt grateful for his observations of the strange land where I also, strangely, found myself, and for insights informed by his multiple perspectives, and his relentlessly questing mind. It is tempting to analyze each essay in this short but densely thoughtful book one by one, but in each of them Miłosz follows through on the multiple implications of the opening sentences of the first essay: "I am here. Those three words contain all that can be said—you begin with those words and you return to them." It is also his intention to begin—as ever—from his own, immediate perceptions rather than from any preconceptions; to "seize naked experience, which eludes all accepted ideas."

(I should reveal that I ended my first book, "*Lost in Translation*, a memoir about emigration and transculturation, with the sentence "I am here now." It is an accidental counterpoint to Miłosz's first sentence in *Visions*, which I didn't become aware of until later and which reinforced my sense of immigrant affinity.)

America, or "this goddamn place," as I sometimes referred to it half in affection, half alienation, was not an easy society or culture to understand. Miłosz's perceptions were informed by a richness of experience unmatched among most writers of his, or any other, era. Still, for him too, America presented its own special challenges: of vastness, of radical newness, of naked nature on an enormous scale. It is clear from his opening essay that he is perfectly aware of the actual geography of California, which he describes evocatively. "But still," he writes, "I find something oppressive in the virginity of this country. . . . Both here, on the West Coast, and everywhere in America, one is faced with something that is impossible to define by allusions to the 'humanistically formed imagination.'" The value of social activity, of cultural distinctions and hierarchies, falls apart in an encounter with the enormousness—and the enormity—of American landscapes, a terrain largely unmarked, and unmarred, by the signposts of recognizable history. "Strangeness, indifference, eternal stone, stone-like eternity, and compared to it, I am a split second of tissue, nerve, pumping heart, and, worst of all, I am subject to the same incomprehensible law ruling what is here before me, which I see only as self-contained and opposed to all meaning," Miłosz writes. He is oddly (although probably inadvertently) echoing an observation made a few decades earlier by D. H. Lawrence, who thought there was something in American landscapes that was inimical to the European man, who arrived on the continent very late, and who was not there by rights or habit.

I don't know if other arrivals from Europe have felt—or continue to feel—the same shock and awe on encountering American nature. Vancouver, which was the site of my first emigration, is spectacularly located several hundred miles up the Pacific Coast from San Francisco, overlooking the Rocky Mountains. The setting is breathtaking and can induce Romantic awe, but when I arrived there, I too felt I was facing too large—and too remote—an expanse. This was undoubtedly a limitation on my part, proceeding from a spatial sense formed by the villages of my childhood and the historically layered beauty of Kraków; intimate spaces one could enter, and in which the presence of the past was palpable.

As usual, however, Miłosz takes his observations further and deeper—to reflections not only on the particulars of Californian flora and fauna but on his relationship to nature altogether. The title "Remembrance of a Certain Love," which he gives to one of his essays, refers to his boyhood love of nature. "When I was a boy," he writes, "I was quite curious about things that ran, flew, and crept, things that grew, things that could be watched and touched, and I had no interest in words." In saying this, he presumably means that he didn't yet have an interest in his future, word-based vocation. He did, however, have an interest in naming and classification, and rather amazingly, given the period in which he was writing *Visions* (long before Foucault, with his theories of knowledge and power), Miłosz identifies this passion as being distinctly masculine: that is, expressing the urge for domination and "the male hunger for demarcations, definitions, and concepts more powerful than reality, a hunger which armed some with swords, cast others into dungeons, and led the faithful on to holy wars."

Even this predilection, however, was complicated by emigration. In America, Miłosz discovers numerous varieties of species that he knew in only one form in his childhood: an enlargement, or a complication of knowledge, in which the singularity, the absoluteness of his first perceptions, is undermined. "I had known only one sort of pine, a pine tree was a pine tree," he writes, "but here suddenly there was the sugar pine, the ponderosa pine, the Monterey pine, and so on—seventeen species, all told." The multiplicity is of course reflected in language, and Miłosz allows himself a rare moment of nostalgia when he contemplates the new species of jay he encounters in California: "Jays screech outside the window (if only they were *sojki*), but they are either California jays or Steller's jays, black on top, blue-breasted with a black crest—only the cries, the thievishness, the audacity are the same as that of their kinsmen thousands of miles away in my native land." This is a form of regretful longing that many emigrants (perhaps especially writers) have known—not only for the landscapes and sights of childhood but for the words which name them, or rather, for a relationship to language that is experienced in childhood, when words seem not only to name but to contain the essence of the things to which they refer. For Miłosz, however many languages he learned and mastered—including Russian, Lithuanian, French, English, and Hebrew—his dedication to poetry was inseparable from his devotion to his native tongue: really, from his dependence on it as a poet. It may be the same bird, but *sojki* for a Polish speaker—and especially a poet—is not the same as "jay," of whatever kind.

The primacy of his first language was never in doubt, but even that was complicated by historical experience. Here's an excerpt from one of his keynote poems, "My Faithful Mother Tongue," written while he was at Berkeley and expressing anguished self-division in his attitudes to Poland and therefore to the Polish language:

Faithful mother tongue,
I have been serving you.

Every night, I used to set before you little
    bowls of colors
so you could have your birch, your cricket,
    your finch
as preserved in my memory. . . .

Now, I confess my doubt.
There are moments when it seems to me I
    have squandered my life,
For you are a tongue of the debased,
of the unreasonable, hating themselves
even more than they hate other nations,
a tongue of informers,
a tongue of the confused,
ill with their own innocence.

But without you, who am I?
Only a scholar in a distant country,
a success, without fears and humiliations.
Yes, who am I without you?
Just a philosopher, like everyone else.

"Without fears and humiliations": one might
think that is a state to be desired, but I think what
Miłosz is pointing to here is that in his "mother
tongue" he experiences things fully. In Polish, he
feels—with all the perils that condition entails,
but also with all the impetus to "felt thought,"
as T. S. Eliot called it. History has complicated

his relationship to the Polish language, but without it, he would be "just a philosopher." Despite the distinctly philosophical tenor of his writing, he didn't want to be a philosopher in the traditional sense, to deal with abstract ideas and theories, either in poetry or in prose. What he wanted instead was language, which served as an instrument for capturing reality—and for him, that was fully possible only in Polish.

Yet even in Polish, "the real" can only be approached, never quite entered. "Life was given but unattainable" is one simple line from a later poem, "Bobo's Metamorphosis," written in 1962, not long after he arrived in California. As in Zeno's paradox, Miłosz keeps trying to attain it in his writing, but life, the thing itself—the *Ding an sich*—cannot be seized, touched, captured in words. Perhaps Miłosz's sense of an unattainable reality—the insatiable hunger of his pansexuality, combined with the more metaphysical urge to grasp "the real" in all its dimensions—is magnified by the condition of exile. This is how many of his poems progress: from specific moments of perception to wonderment about the nature of reality in which we humans live, on all its levels.

In the very different mode of prose, this is also the progression of *Visions from San Francisco Bay*. After the essays proceeding from the astonishment of his first encounters with Californian nature, Miłosz presses on to take questions of nature further—not so much to the heights of abstraction as to primary, underlying modes of understanding. In the essay "On the Effects of the Natural Sciences," he looks at how the changing metaphors of the natural world affect our very understanding of who we are. From God the creator, to God the Great Watchmaker, to Mother Nature, and, finally, to evolution and "Movement: of galaxies, atoms, the parts of the atom, explosions, dislocations, transformation": in Miłosz's expansive vision, our conceptions of the universe in which we live shape, however consciously or otherwise, our sense of human nature and its possibilities.

The notion of "movement," which pervades everything from the astonishing activities of ants to the motion of the planets, becomes one of Miłosz's governing concepts—a preoccupation perhaps also affected by his own experience of profound change. For him, this includes the temporal movement of evolution from cellular forms to mammals: a progression in which humans come to be seen as part of nature, albeit one distinguished by exceptional traits. The human being, in Miłosz's very contemporary conception, is a mammal that produces "morality and law . . . as a genus, just as beets produce sugar." The argument of the essay is complicated, but Miłosz doesn't want to accept the idea of the person as *only* natural. Humans are, on one hand, part of nature, but what American nature reveals to him vividly is that the natural world is both mysterious and without human significance. The suffering of animals, which he is acutely aware of, is different from human suffering. For one thing, human meanings—including a sense of pleasure and pain—emanate not only from the body but also from our mental lives. For Miłosz, that means the crucial difference between humans and other living creatures inheres in *Homo sapiens'* understanding of right and wrong—or, with a more religious inflection, of good and evil. In his view, an intrinsic moral sense is as inescapable as our knowledge— exceptional in the animal kingdom—that we will die. This too is an awareness that urges us to make sense of our lives and to strive for something more than mere survival (Freud would have agreed).

Californian nature, in its forbidding otherness, holds important, if disturbing, knowledge and brings him back to fundamental questions. But perhaps more crucially, in the country Miłosz newly encounters, the inner space within that exceptional human species is ineluctably alienated. Alienation was of course one of the master concepts of the American sixties, and Miłosz goes on to comment on it in various ways; but in his initial, quite distinctive analysis, the estrangement he feels in California has to do, surprisingly, not with nature but with physical spaces of the human-made, built environment. His reactions to this aspect of place are informed, quite explicitly, by his perspective from the Other Europe. "The people I now live among could never guess that I come from a place without automobiles, bathrooms, or telephones, that on our roads . . . five miles was a considerable distance, and people managed without doctors, trusting instead to home remedies, charms, and spells." So he writes in an essay titled "A Certain Illness Difficult to Name." But now he finds himself in the land of endless highways and skyscrapers, whose size and anonymity, in his view, contribute to the enigmatic illness. He eventually identifies this elusive disorder as "ontological anemia"—a brilliant phrase for a condition that many immigrants would have recognized, without being able to name it or diagnose its causes. Miłosz is speaking here of certain shortages of selfhood, an internal emptiness, which he attributes not only to frontier individualism but to the ungraspable hugeness of American spaces. "No one will ever succeed in defining happiness," he writes, "but certainly one of its conditions is that a certain modest scale not be overstepped." In other words, what Miłosz misses—what so many who came from "elsewhere" either consciously or less articulately missed—is a sense of intimacy: with one's environment, with other people, and perhaps most crucially with oneself. When I first read Miłosz's essays, which deal, more or less explicitly, with the roots of American identity in successive European migrations, I felt a sense both of recognition and gratitude. He dared to say what I think many immigrants have secretly felt about the country that promised so much— no less than "the American Dream"—but so often delivered anxieties, loneliness, and that inadmissible sense of estrangement. The migrants who left the impoverished parts of Italy or eastern Europe in great numbers did so for good reasons; their lives were materially miserable. But in "the old country" they had something they could not find in America: they had each other. Crucially, their poverty was shared, and "their work had been incorporated into the rituals of a community with traditions, beliefs, and the blessings of neighbors." Possibly, there is an element of idealization in Miłosz's analysis here, but for those immigrants who didn't "make it" in America, the difference between shared poverty and shameful individual impoverishment was something they experienced on their skin, together with a strange unhappiness they could not fully understand or admit.

But Miłosz, as always, wants to avoid nostalgia. He is well aware that Europe was also changing as he wrote, that traffic-filled roads were beginning to connect charming hillside towns of Italy, and that on the way to medieval cathedrals housing glorious art, you could pass urban developments of surpassing ugliness. That is, he knows that the place where he lives, with its anonymous high-ways and habitations, is on the sharp cutting edge of a wider change. He declares that it is therefore "a privilege to participate in America, just as once, in the cities devastated by the totalitarian plague, I thought that, if I survived, I would be richer with the knowledge whose absence impairs the educa-tion of my contemporaries." Extremity is instruc-tive, as is a cross-cultural perspective, and Miłosz's education leads to the realization that America, for better or worse, stands for the future. It is the place where, he concludes, "this century attains its full insanity."

If America was the future, California was its cutting edge. But in *Visions*, Miłosz shows himself to be impressively aware (as so many were not) that the place where he has so strangely arrived also has a past, however different it was from European versions of history. He speaks of California's early inhabitants' encounters with formidable nature, but also the attempts of Mexican missionaries to impose Christianity on Indians without recognizing their particular forms of culture or identity; he identifies a history marked by wars against the same Native inhabitants, which, he adds in a comment still resonant today, were "wars only for the Indians defending themselves. For the white men they were police actions against criminals whose guilt was proven in advance." California's history, in his telling, includes a pioneer story of the Gold Rush and cowboy conquests, later represented in movie westerns, hugely popular at the time Miłosz was writing. He understands that the violence of the far West included slave deals with Hawaii and Russian attempts to establish a fur-trading presence; above all (as those westerns often showed), that it was marked by devil-may-care liberty to kill or be killed without inconvenient interventions of the law or still barely existent institutions.

For a late arrival from a distant part of the world, Miłosz's willingness to study California's past is impressive. But it is the present—or the hyperpresent—on which most of the essays in *Visions* concentrate. Given that from a street in Berkeley he can see "the nuclear laboratories glowing among the eucalyptus trees," that the skyscrapers and bridges of San Francisco are nearby, Miłosz is of course aware that the civilization in which he finds himself is highly advanced technologically, that it is the gold standard of a certain kind of progress, whose forms are so new and unexpected that they are outpacing our usual categories of perception. In an interestingly paradoxical diagnosis, the ubiquity of the technological layer covering the American ground means, in his view, that American civilization "appears to be Nature itself, endowed with nearly all the features of that other nature." A kind of second nature, in other words, whose carapace covers the first—and that is just as forbidding and "impenetrable in its opposition to meaning" as the great, untamed expanses of American wilderness.

These days, it is easy to feel that the internet, with its vast inclusiveness, is almost a new kind and layer of nature, covering the world in which we live. But Miłosz was writing well before that, addressing America itself as a kind of demiurge, from which a new world was emerging. Aside from its political power—huge at the time he was writing—he notes the sheer size of the country, its parts connected by those anonymous highways along which he sometimes traveled, encountering, between the great metropolises of the East and West coasts, nothing more than small outcroppings of architecturally rudimentary, and mostly friendless, towns. (I well remember car trips along the endless, monotonous ribbons of those highways, and the deep chill I occasionally felt as I traversed the great solitary expanses, now and then encountering other moving capsules, with their lone inhabitants enclosed within.)

In a sense, many of the essays on American nature and the material world can be read as Miłosz's attempt to analyze the sources of his own alienation—different in degree and kind from his anger at the French intellectual establishment. Altogether, alienation is of course very different from anger; it springs from a more ineffable inner distance, rather than from conscious opposition to an adversary. This is undoubtedly why Miłosz could combine genuine gratitude to America with a deep critique of some of its cultural features. And this may also be why his observations of Californian culture—and especially its brand-new counterculture—remain, even now, startling in their insights. His observations of the latter phenomenon take up a large portion of *Visions* and strike me, in his refusal to be either scandalized by its more far-out aspects or to be properly "cool," as penetrating on a deeper level. The sharpest angle of vision is often oblique.

Indeed, for someone who came to California in late middle life and whose main task was teaching Slavic literature, Miłosz was impressively aware of the eccentric phenomena arising there, in forms that were often strange or shocking to most of his peers, and even to the more conventional members of my own, baby-boom generation. He knows, for example, that California is "a mecca for seekers of mystical unity, for consciousness-expanding drugs, ecstatic sects, publications devoted to Hinduism and Zen Buddhism, for prophets preaching wisdom borrowed from Tibetan monks"—tendencies that make it, in his view, "the capital of everything that is turning against Western man's fondness for intellectual precision." The turn to Eastern mysticism, as he understands it, arises from a wish to dissolve the boundaries of the self—that American self, which seemed so enigmatically troubled—in a quest to blend with . . . what? That, of course, was often unclear to Western adepts of Eastern religions themselves, but dissolving that inadequate ordinary self by "opening the doors of perception"—a phrase coined by no less an intellectual than Aldous Huxley—was also the goal of taking psychedelic drugs, with their often disturbing effects.

Perhaps his fullest and most personal response to the turn toward Eastern religions comes in his poem "To Raja Rao," addressed to a near-contemporary Indian writer living in Austin,

Texas—that is, another countercultural mecca—
who studied Catholic theology and taught philosophy. Here are a few excerpts from the long,
moving poem, dated Berkeley, 1969:

> Raja, I wish I knew
> the cause of that malady.
>
> For years I could not accept
> the place I was in.
> I felt I should be somewhere else. . . .
>
> Somewhere else there was a city of real
>   presence,
> of real trees and voices and friendship and
>   love. . . .
>
> Ill at ease in the tyranny, ill at ease in the
>   republic,
> in the one I longed for freedom, in the
>   other for the end of corruption. . . .
>
> I learned at last to say: this is my home,
> here, before the glowing coal of ocean
>   sunsets,
> on the shore which faces the shores of your
>   Asia,
> in a great republic, moderately corrupt. . . .
>
> I hear you saying that liberation is possible
> and that Socratic wisdom
> is identical with your guru's.

No, Raja, I must start from what I am.
I am those monsters which visit my dreams
And reveal to me my hidden essence. . . .

No help, Raja, my part is agony,
struggle, abjection, self-love, and self-hate,
prayer for the Kingdom
and reading Pascal.

"My part is agony": this is more directly confessional than the temper of most of Miłosz's poems; perhaps in addressing the poem to Rao, he felt that he was speaking to a worthy interlocutor who might understand his philosophical allusions, and his European-bred, anti-utopian conception of what it means to be human. Internal conflict and struggle, troubling dreams, something that might be called the unconscious—these, to Miłosz, are aspects of being a particular person: of being himself. Perhaps one can say that however much he accepted the place he was in—"a great republic, moderately corrupt"—he didn't want to leave his first, European self: an identity grounded in more traditional cultures, with all their tenets of individuality, and their guideposts to being a person. Guideposts that could be repressive, and could lead to guilt, shame, emotional and intellectual struggles—but which left you in no doubt as to who you were.

The various meditational cults of California, with their costumes, chants, and proselytizing excesses, were a well-known sixties phenomenon. But Miłosz finds the drive to depersonalization paradoxically present in more unexpected aspects of the counterculture—beginning with what might be called the sexualization of everyday life. In "Sex Provided," he analyzes the various manifestations of "the sexual myth" in the media, in advertising, and in mass nudity he witnessed on some beaches. He reads a Berkeley rag called *The Barb*, which delivers "fifteen minutes of hate" aimed at the nonhip in every issue. (I wonder how many other faculty members would have been acquainted with this local publication.) He notes the newspaper's "cult of romantic figures—Fidel Castro, Che Guevara, Ho Chi Minh"—and its insouciant descriptions of sex gatherings or, not to put too fine a point on it, orgies. He examines its ads for sexual services, offered in this case not by female "sex workers" but by men, for a quoted fee. He notes that *The Barb*'s combination of sex and outrage is a successful business formula, adopted, in milder versions, by other magazines, and he adds, quite presciently, that "we cannot be sure that the editors of all those 'Barbs' will not end their careers as smiling priests of Moloch." Indeed, quite a few of them did.

The new forms of sexual freedom were a frequent subject of critique and feminist debates from within American culture itself; but Miłosz, as usual, goes further and probes deeper than most critics in analyzing the implications of sex being so ubiquitously available, and the perfect orgasm being its great desideratum. The problem, in his view, is not so much specific visual or literary pornography but the idea that sex is divorced from relationships, in all their complexity and difficulty: that it is purely an act of the body, rather than the psyche and mind. Interestingly, he points out that in the literary dystopias by Huxley, Orwell, and the less well-known Russian writer Zamyatin, sex is a permitted diversion—as opposed to "the passions, which draw persons, not bodies, together and engage them both as flesh and as spirit." Passions are dangerous because they carry personal meanings that escape totalitarian control and because they reveal the reduction of the individual to mindless physiology, not as liberation, but "as slavery."

I don't think Miłosz's critique should be mistaken for the opinions of someone belonging to a repressed or "uptight" older generation. The "generation gap," much discussed in the sixties, doesn't apply in this cross-cultural case. Miłosz may have been discreet about his own relationships, but he was not, either in his writing, or, most probably, in his life, puritanical. In fact, his discretion may be a confirmation of the very values he is espousing in his critique of "sexual liberation." His private relationships were private; they were personal, not meant for mass consumption.

Indeed, if I first read these reflections, too, with a sense of recognition, that was because of my sense that the much-vaunted sexual revolution in the United States played itself out in specifically American terms. For the baby-boom generation (to which I belonged chronologically, if not always in spirit), "sexual liberation" was an attempt to overthrow 1950s puritanism and an inversion of all its terms—which, like all such revolts, left traces of the rejected object intact. Among other things, I was baffled by the problematization of sex and sexuality among my peers; the anxieties about attractiveness I discovered among my women friends; the fear of intimacy among young men; and, in another vein, the relentless and often crude emphasis on male sexual prowess in the novels of such literary greats as Saul Bellow, Philip Roth, or Norman Mailer. Was sex really invented in 1963, as Philip Larkin told us? It didn't seem so, where I had come from. Polish culture, for all its Catholic underpinnings, was not puritanical about sex, and its notions of what was "feminine" and "masculine" were not as polarized as those obtaining in post-war America. This is not to say that women achieved complete equality with their male counterparts, but they were not left out of the professions, or of those long-night conversations around the kitchen table in which the day's issues could be honestly discussed. Camaraderie between men and women was a real possibility, and so was women's participation in political movements, leading from nineteenth-century uprisings all the way to Solidarity. This was very different from the American situation, where the fifties were a particularly puritanical period. If "second wave" feminism originated in the United States, that was surely because, within its cultural context, it was much needed.

Miłosz, of course, in addition to his powers of observation and analysis, had a vast historical vision, and he understood, as most hip young Americans did not, that the countercultural rebellions had precedents in Europe. In an essay entitled "The Agony of the West," he traces both the catastrophism and the utopianism he discerns in American hippiedom to various movements—both artistic and political—bred on the old continent. The premise of this complicated essay is that "A conviction of the decadence, the rotting of the West, seems to be a permanent part of the equipment of enlightened and sensitive people for dealing with the horrors accompanying technological progress." This is most pronounced "in the country that has achieved the greatest economic power in history, but where—judging by the rage and contempt emanating from books, paintings, and films—never before have so many people taken up indictment as a pastime." In looking for precursors of prophetic condemnation, he cites Rousseau, Tolstoy, the Romantics, Marxist alienation, and—importantly in his worldview—the deification of art as a substitute for religion.

Still, 1960s America was not nineteenth-century Europe, and in between were the actual events of the Terrible Century, which, in Miłosz's view, brought on "an orgy, a pandemonium" of self-disgust, justified in "fashionable discourses on *la nausée*, the absurd, alienation." He may have been thinking of Sartre (who, after all, wrote a book called *Nausea*) and his cohort, but he also saw such attitudes being adopted by hip American rebels, disgusted with their own mainstream, work-and-money-driven culture. Certainly, "alienation" was one of the keynote terms of my generation, and it covered a multitude of sins. It also led to various antidotes, including the radical gestures of "dropping out" or joining hippie communes, which for a while sprouted in various bucolic settings, and which, in Miłosz's view, were an attempt to re-create American versions of Arcadia, originating in the writings of Whitman and Thoreau. American radicals, with their visions of idyllic utopias, were in Miłosz's diagnosis often backward-looking rather than Marxist in their "revolutionary" ideas. And of course, the communes often became riddled with conflict, or turned darkly dystopian, as in the Manson family cult.

To my immigrant self, at a time when I wished ardently to establish some new sense of "the normal"—a comprehensible sense of human personality and reality in an American vein—such *in vivo* experiments that people performed on themselves seemed perplexing and sometimes quite frightening. My first close encounters with life- and self-alteration took place at Rice University, in Houston, Texas, where I spent the mid-1960s, and where the countercultural rebellions were aided by the easy availability of drugs, imported from nearby Mexico. I was also witnessing a head-on clash between the very conservative mainstream culture of Texas and the brave new counterculture. There were reports not only of ecstatic but of very bad trips, of severe emotional disorders, and of students being briefly imprisoned. At the further extremes, some students from small Texan towns were literally driven mad by the juxtaposition of their fundamentalist upbringing and the university's culture of secular humanism. A few began speaking in tongues; a group of students who for some reason decided I was "one of them" was eventually forced to leave the university because of pistols and knives found in their possession—arms they were collecting for a potential invasion from Cuba, which they predicted by telepathic means. Yet others decided to give up on the "rat race" and drop out altogether, devoting themselves to opening the doors of their perceptions ever wider. "I saw the best minds of my generation destroyed by madness," Allen Ginsberg said, and Miłosz knew the American poet's work well. It should be added, however, that quite a few of the dropouts eventually took up professional lives, sometimes doing very well, as they turned from various experiments in alternative living to life as an all-too-real project.

When I eventually read *Visions*, its insights were a consolation as well as an education. By analogy with the concept of "thick description," proposed by the anthropologist Clifford Geertz as a way to understand other cultures, Miłosz offers thick perception. Each essay in the book is a small feat of condensed observation and thought, but, at the same time, their progression traces the U-shaped trajectory of Miłosz's own perspective. He begins with observations of America made, implicitly, from his European point of view; approximately at the book's midpoint, in "The Agony of the West," his insights glide back and forth between America and Europe; but from then on his vantage point largely shifts again, and in a subsequent essay, "The Formless and the New," he writes, implicitly, as someone who is explaining American realities to outsiders, from within. "If I did not live here," he begins, "where fashions, both intellectual and otherwise, originate and then spread across the whole of America . . . I would be less certain that something still unnamed and absolutely new is now emerging." The generic name he gives to the phenomenon is "Hippieland," and it is astonishing, really, how closely, from his newly American perspective, he is willing to observe it, and how seriously he thinks about it. He understands, for example, the hip embrace of Indian fashions and of narcotics originally used in Indian rituals—in other words, an embrace of the internal exotic. And he wonders what happens if the distinction "between political subversive, vagabond, student, poet, singer of original ballads, and even Indian is erased, as it was for the hippies whom I picked up hitchhiking on Euclid Avenue recently?"

This is an interesting glimpse of Miłosz himself: game enough, or curious enough, to pick up hippie hitchhikers on a street named—with wonderful irony—Euclid Avenue. But if he sees Hippieland as something different (after all) from various European versions of Bohemia, including postwar existentialism, that is partly because the American version, in his view, is not a marginal phenomenon but "one of the symptoms of America's split into two mutually hostile parts." In other words, this is wholesale, significant cultural change, and Miłosz seeks its roots not only in "culture," as it is usually understood, but in what to him are the all-important material causes. He takes into account the view of some liberal commentators that the appearance of the counterculture "corresponds exactly in time with the onset of automation, which will deprive ever larger numbers of people of work"—although in some of Hippiedom's more utopian visions, "the state will guarantee everyone a decent pension." This is oddly close to working-class worries about increasing automation of work in present-day America—concerns that were to a considerable extent responsible for Donald Trump's improbable victory in the 2016 presidential race. The utopian solutions offered in Miłosz's time have also been echoed by some contemporary prescriptions for a much shorter working day and a guaranteed amount of money given to all citizens, regardless of whether they are employed or not. It has to be said that Miłosz is rather more perceptive than most proponents of well-paid unemployment, noting that "for the average American citizen . . . freedom from all work would threaten madness." He also notes that Black Americans, so often deprived of work against their will, did not always sympathize with "the longhairs" in their advocacy of dropping out or other life experiments and opinions.

Eventually, in order to understand hip rebellions with all their strange manifestations, or at least to find some analogies for them, Miłosz turns his vision almost beyond Europe, to its eastern edges, and the revolt of the Russian intelligentsia in the nineteenth century. Like early Russian revolutionaries, the ostensibly radical Berkeley students donning Indian headbands and adopting Black slang, or shouting down the university's quite liberal president at a Free Speech rally that Miłosz attended (again, I wonder how many of his fellow faculty members did so), "were united by the tacit and, for them, obvious premise that any authority issuing from the evil system . . . was itself pure evil." The great difference between the two "revolutions" was that the Berkeley rebellions were almost entirely costless: no gulag, no Lubyanka prison, no Siberian exile.

Undoubtedly, the costlessness of 1960s rebellions added to the sense of their frivolity: young people dressing up, getting high, and playing other, ostensibly serious games without any grave consequences. But it seems to me that for all his insights into such phenomena, Miłosz, in his search for metacultural and material causes of the rebellions, may have missed their roots in something more ordinary: the aridity of everyday, middle-class American life. I'm not sure how much, from his Berkeley perch, he had seen of it, but had he been acquainted with the great stretches of suburbia flanking the cities on both coasts, with their prosperous, self-enclosed houses, their almost entire absence of pedestrians, their chilling lack of family intimacy, their work-driven, inarticulate fathers and their house-bound, all too often alcohol-tippling mothers, he might have observed that other form of alienation: not from politics or society at large, but from middle-class versions of self and feeling, with their oddly reduced idea of what it meant to be a person. Think about the world of Updike, or Salinger, or even *Mad Men*—that brilliant television rendition of American malaise in the 1950s and the radical reactions against it in the subsequent decade—for glimpses of that American world.

Nevertheless, although he is bemused, to put it mildly, by some of Hippieland's more far-out antics, Miłosz doesn't discount its emerging culture entirely. For example, he rather surprisingly sug-

gests that the use of marijuana is quite harmless—
and that the rear-guard actions undertaken by the
police against it were less an attempt to address a
real problem than a symptom of defensiveness on
the part of mainstream America. Moreover, the
criminalization of marijuana had, in his eyes,
the paradoxically beneficial effect of "causing the
whites to draw nearer the blacks." To be a crimi-
nal means to look at society from the bottom,
from underground, the way it is seen by Blacks,
who know the color of their skin "makes them
suspicious to the police." Given that he was a
relatively new observer of such matters, this is a
surprisingly astute comment. Indeed, Miłosz's
sensitivity to issues of racial prejudice is threaded
throughout his essays, and perhaps, in an indirect way, this too can be attributed to his cross-
cultural perspective. Prewar Poland had its quota
of prejudices, directed at minority populations,
which included large numbers of Ukrainians,
ethnic Germans, and of course Jews—with anti-
Semitism being the most prevalent form of bigotry. But I think an argument can be made that
in Miłosz's formative years, Poland was free of
racism, simply because nonwhite people were
almost entirely absent from its territory; instead, they were known from the fictions of Karl
May, and some charming, if perhaps exoticizing,
children's poetry. To attribute lack of racism to

this absence is perhaps not very ennobling, but I think it can be fairly said that Miłosz's perceptions of racial prejudice—whether it was directed at Blacks or Native Americans—came from first-hand observations and genuine sympathies, rather than any form of political correctness.

Miłosz's mind, his imagination, were capacious; he was certainly not going to be shocked by the new bohemians. In fact, at times he contemplates them with a kind of wonderment, as in a poem called "The Year" dated Berkeley, 1963:

> I looked around in the unknown year,
>   aware that few are those
>   who come from so far, I was saturated
>   with sunlight as a plant
>   with water.
> That was a high year, fox-colored, like a
>   crosscut redwood stump
>   or vine leaves on the hills in November.
> In its groves and chambers the pulse of
>   music was beating strongly,
>   running down from dark mountains,
>   tributaries entangled.
> A generation clad in patterned robes
>   trimmed with little bells
>   greeted me with the banging of conga
>   drums.

I repeated their guttural songs of ecstatic
    despair walking by the sea
      when it bore in boys on surfboards and
        washed my footprints away.
At the very border of inhabited time the
    same lessons were being
      learned, how to walk on two legs and to
        pronounce the signs
      traced in the always childish book of our
        species.
I would have related, had I known how,
    everything which a single
    memory can gather for the praise of men.
O sun, o stars, I was saying, holy, holy, holy
    is our being beneath
    heaven and the day and our endless
      communion.

"The Year" is an intensely sensuous poem, in which the music of time and space are interchangeable, and in which Californian nature now has not only awesomeness but its own, lyrical beauty. Miłosz contemplates the temporal as well as geographical distance he has traveled to arrive "at the very border of inhabited time"— where, nevertheless, he recognizes the same human condition, with all its childishness and wonder.

"The Year" can be read as one possible summation of Miłosz's response to Californian counterculture. But in *Visions*, after dissecting Hippiedom's symptoms and syndromes, he shifts the direction of his gaze yet again. In the essay called "The Evangelical Emissary," he begins the inversion with an odd figure nicknamed "Holy Hubert," whom he observes preaching at the entrance to the Berkeley campus. Again, it is evidence of Miłosz's willingness to take on the marginal and the apparently insignificant that he applies to this rather pathetic personage his full analytic powers. Hubert is seen by Berkeley students as a harmless figure of fun, but Miłosz discerns in him something more meaningful: "a delegate from the traditional morality sent out among the apostates and sinners." He should be preaching in Arkansas or Kentucky, where he would undoubtedly find some followers; in Berkeley he only serves to illustrate "the erosion of the system of ideas and customs which form the American way of life."

For Miłosz, the juxtaposition of Holy Hubert with Hippieland helped him understand the country's deep lines of division. The idea that the United States is actually two countries, however the differences are parsed—North and South, working class and rich, Black and white, the coasts and the great middle—continues to this day, and Miłosz concludes his short but observation-packed essay with a sentence that could perhaps only be penned by an outsider, un-implicated in the culture wars by belonging to one or the other camp: "If it were up to me," he writes, "I would prefer not to be forced to choose between them."

It was undoubtedly a perceptual advantage of his outsider position that, in fact, he didn't have to choose, and that he could contemplate various manifestations of American life with an equal measure of detachment and insight. In an essay titled "I, Motor, Earth," he turns his attention—by then informed both by Europe and California—toward the enormous expanses of land between the two coasts. The essay is partly a meditation on that great icon of American identity and the not so discreet object of (especially male) desire: the automobile. What interests Miłosz is not the car itself, how-ever, but the process of moving across America in its enclosed capsule, along the country's end-less highways. If such a trip is a very different experience from travel across say, Italy or France, that is not only because the country he traverses is so huge but because the landscapes of the great American middle are so sparsely inhab-ited and the layer of human-made structures so provisional and thin. Where are the beautiful towns of Umbria, the lovely villages of Périgord, the medieval streets of English towns? Miłosz disavows nostalgia, but surely such comparisons are embedded in his mind as he passes through "those little towns which are like nomad camps, so impermanent, so makeshift are their walls of painted plywood and neon."

Yet it is the inhabitants of these towns who elicit his most mixed feelings. As he contemplates an impeccably made-up waitress preparing hamburgers in a "Desert Center," he admits feeling "undeserved superiority" to her and other "mental cripples" he encounters in the small towns. The condescending scorn of the phrase is rare in his writings and clearly troubling; eventually, in lieu of such personal reactions, he finds what he always needs when confronting new realities: a more systemic, and at the same time more concrete, explanation. The inhabitants of middle America, he concludes, spend their lives working, often in dull and meaningless jobs, and this does not allow them "to break through their habits of mind." There is also the nefarious influence of television and roadside ads, "which become richer in brutality and more moronic, the further one goes from the big cities." And no bookstores anywhere in sight, no time (or urge) to read.

I remember the constriction of soul, an almost frightening sense of inner emptiness, as I occasionally traveled through Texas, with its expanses of arid wilderness, dotted with outcroppings of rudimentary human settlements. From my experience at Rice University, I knew that many of their inhabitants were fundamentalist in their religion, proud gun owners, and hyperconservative in their opinions. On stopping at a café once with a Texan companion, I found it very difficult to talk to its owners or its other, monosyllabic customers. But I think that in looking for explanations of such inarticulate silences, Miłosz underestimated the provinciality of middle America and many of its inhabitants' lack of curiosity about the wider world. In 1990 only 10 percent of all Americans owned passports or had been outside their country. The number has now increased but is still well below 50 percent. Why this lack of interest, this narrowing of human possibility? Part of the problem was (and continues to be) the dearth of good education for so many. But on the political level, this form of provinciality may have to do with the conviction, which has persisted so stubbornly among large portions of the population, that America is the norm to which the rest of the world should aspire. For the inhabitants of small-town America whom Miłosz encountered in the 1960s who had never visited the more "decadent" urban centers, let alone any other country, America was simply the best country in the world; there was no need to step outside it or to take an interest in other, inferior places.

Miłosz's own diagnostic uncertainty continues to show in the chapter's vacillations. After commenting on middle America, the direction of his thought turns yet again towards the "long-hairs"—this time in the guise of angry young poets—and the cultural sources of "on the road" literature and films. "I understand what pains American youth, so full of hatred, so promethean and romantic," he writes, and quotes a Parisian intellectual who summed up her impressions after driving across America in a devastating phrase: *"Mon Dieu, quel malheur."*

My god, what misfortune. That is a European's comment, but from the nineteenth century on, there has also been a considerable body of American literature analyzing various forms of such misery: American nervousness, American loneliness, American violence, "The Culture of American Narcissism," and, shortly following, "The Culture of Complaint." The malaise of the American soul—whether it was attributed to frontier individualism, an excessive work ethic, or the turn to countercultural self-indulgence—

was a phenomenon noticed by many American commentators as well as visitors from abroad.

Still, Miłosz cannot rest with his own disaffection or snobbishness, and he doesn't want to come down on the side of the hip and the privileged against the inarticulate "silent majority." Almost parenthetically, he remembers "a young simpleton" in California who asked him "how life in Sacramento differed from life in a concentration camp." This is ignorance equal to that of the silent waitress—and perhaps less justifiable. "The simpleton" was making a hip "radical" comment rather than no comment at all. But he, too, lacked any imagination of difference: in circumstances, in degrees of suffering, in ways of being human.

Miłosz, of course, possessed multiple perspectives, and in another attempt to arrive at a more affirmative appraisal of the country he lives in, he suggests that "overall, auto trips about America result in admiration for man, and compassion." This is something he always strives for: in this case, his admiration is for the sheer accomplishment of covering the "geological monster" of American spaces with highways and erecting motels "in a wild landscape," which offer "clean bedsheets, a comfortable bed, a bathroom with hot water." (Perhaps this too is to some extent informed by a European—or specifically eastern

European—perspective. Certainly, after experiencing the primitive domestic utilities of postwar Poland, I often felt that the availability of a hot shower, wherever you found yourself, was one of the great American achievements.)

And then, more turns still. Was all this achieved "at the cost of their minds"? He means here those ordinary small-town Americans, and he avers that he certainly wouldn't want to end up like them. And what about the costs of destroying nature? "A lover of the forest, I turn my eyes away from the hideous destruction on the mountain slopes where the saws have passed. The ecological balance destroyed, this forest will never grow back." This is certainly advanced for his time. But then, in another qualification, Miłosz implies that this too is the cost of development, which has to be accepted. "It is easy to see," he inconclusively concludes, "that the automobile multiplies our questions because it allows us to be ubiquitous."

In a sense, "I, Motor, Earth" is one of the most revealing of Miłosz's American essays, and the "I" of the title suggests why. In most of his writing, he drives from observation to reflection and, through it, to pursuing fundamental reasons, root causes, and the broadest possible contexts for the phenomena he describes. Here, he includes himself, with all his vacillations, judgments, and personal responses to what he observes and experiences. Perhaps what one senses in the essay's unresolved ambiguities is that for all his gratitude to America and his admiration of the United States, he didn't find it a comfortable country to live in, and a lingering sense of estrangement—creatively so fruitful and personally so difficult—never entirely left him.

The essays in *Visions* record Miłosz's travels in space and his shifts of geographical and cultural perspective, but the poetry that emerges from his Californian years often records his travels in time. Writing from the cutting edge of the present, he often turns to the vanished past. After all, the places where he grew up, and the many people he loved and lost, exist only in memory—his memory. Miłosz once remarked to me in conversation that geographical distance increases the sense of distance in time, and the longing to bridge that divide, to touch on the disappeared places and people, leads to some of his most poignant poems. Here are a few passages from "Elegy for N. N.":

> Tell me if it is too far for you.
> You could have run over the small waves of
> the Baltic
> and past the fields of Denmark, past a beech
> wood . . .

The Sacramento River could have led you
between hills overgrown with prickly oaks.
Then just a eucalyptus grove, and you had
    found me.

True, when the manzanita is in bloom
and the bay is clear on spring mornings
I think reluctantly of the house between
    the lakes
and of nets drawn in beneath the
    Lithuanian sky. . . .

How could one live at that time, I really
    can't say.
Styles and dresses flicker, indistinct,
not self-sufficient, tending toward a finale.
Does it matter that we long for things as
    they are in themselves? . . .

We learned so much, this you know well:
how, gradually, what could not be taken
    away
is taken. People, countrysides.
And the heart does not die when one
    thinks it should,
we smile, there is tea and bread on the
    table.
And only remorse that we did not love
the poor ashes in Sachsenhausen
with absolute love, beyond human power.

The sense of pure heartache is palpable here, and so is the longing for the impossible: to revive the past, to bring back someone, something he loved. It is also poignant in the extreme to think of Miłosz traveling across those unbridgeable imaginative distances from a place where so few knew about or would have understood his history, to the sites of so much loss and death.

It is one of the consequences of emigration—especially across such great cultural as well as geographical divides—that one loses the possibility of shared memory and, therefore, of sharing its burdens. Transplantation to a place as radically different as Berkeley was from Miłosz's cultural origins and early experiences entailed, among other things, an exile from his past. In juxtaposition with his essays on the hipsters of Berkeley or the inhabitants of America's small towns, one can begin to sense, in poems such as "Elegy for N. N.," what must have been an essential loneliness—however much he avoided such self-pitying terms and ways of thinking about his experience.

"Does it matter that we long for things as they are in themselves?" Especially in relation to a vanished past, it is an impossible longing, and one can sense in the question the burden of feeling implicit in it. But also perhaps the hope that the fidelity of memory—and honoring of the particular—carries within itself the possibility of redemptive powers. Memory, for Miłosz, especially from the war onward, was and remained a moral imperative, as in a poem about Miss Jadwiga, "A little hunchback, librarian by profession," who perished in the rubble of Warsaw during the uprising and who is no longer remembered by anyone ("Six Lectures in Verse"). The poem finishes with a kind of credo:

> The little skeleton of Miss Jadwiga, the spot
> Where her heart was pulsating. This only
> I set against necessity, law, theory.

The past is untouchable, but its meanings are clear. The present is visible and concrete, but its structures, its conflicts, the forces that shape it, are difficult to discern. Perhaps this is why the essays in *Visions* progress from reflections on specific, observable phenomena of American life to an analysis of the underlying principles and forces shaping the American present. One of these principles is what Miłosz calls "virtue"—although his definition of it (in the essay titled "On Virtue") is eccentric and sometimes, it must be admitted, abstract to the point of opaqueness. "Virtue" has nothing to do with moral (or Christian) notions of goodness, or kindness, or doing unto others as you would have them do unto you. Rather, in a more Roman definition, it inheres in "courage, resolve, persever-ance, control of the constantly changing emo-tions and impulses." Virtue is strength, and strength is what we need to grapple with na-ture, which is not "a loving mother but ravages and kills us without qualms." (Was he thinking of Californian fires, with their long history?) The quality of virtue has been exercised by "leaders and soldiers, torturers and the tortured, saints and criminals, captains and crews, owners and workers." I confess that the far-reaching moral equivalence implicit in this list doesn't seem to me to stand up to scrutiny, and I wonder whether the ardent admiration Miłosz expresses in the essay for the courage of young soldiers in World War I, no matter which side they were on, suggests some lingering guilt for not hav-ing fought in his time's defining conflict: for eluding death and not achieving an impossible rescue.

But the real point of the essay is that "The United States is a land of virtue." Indeed, virtue, as Miłosz understands it, is in his view a pre-eminently American quality, through which the United States established its independence, and which characterized both sides in the Civil War. Virtue also inheres in the work ethic (which was still alive and well in his time), and it enables America to produce new technologies and machines—including, in a prophetically futuristic vision, "machines that produce other machines that produce other machines." But virtue—at least in this conception of it—also involves self-denial, repression, sometimes Ahab's madness in *Moby-Dick*, or even the rise of Hitler, brought to power by "one of the most virtuous people, the Germans."

The oscillations of Miłosz's perceptions suggest both a complex vision and a deep ambivalence about the country to which fate has brought him, but he eventually finds a kind of resolution of his own conflicts in the improbable setting of American country fairs. I doubt that many members of the American intelligentsia would have contemplated attending such events. For them, as for countercultural radicals, the fairs probably represented "nothing more than the dull, insipid life of yokels and provincial boors." But Miłosz likes "the parades with the American flag, the horses, the decorated saddles inlaid with silver (his observations, as always, are exact), a band wearing false noses, the pom-pom girls," and other aspects of folksy Americana, which so annoyed the "revolutionaries," and would have surely seemed utterly exotic (or irredeemably vulgar) to his European readers. What he really appreciates at the fairs, though, as he does with great consistency throughout his writing, is the "virtue" of agricultural work they celebrate and the frameworks that allow it—which, he notes, can be so easily ruined. He is surely thinking of the *kolkhozy* and the farm collectives that brought so much suffering to the peasants of eastern Europe and destroyed so much of that region's agriculture. Again, the knowledge of destruction is a standard against which humble, ordinary human activity gains its value, and even a certain beauty.

It is difficult to summarize Miłosz's views on America gathered in a chapter called "Emigration to America: A Summing Up," since his reflections in this case mostly take place at a level of abstraction that sometimes verges on the impenetrable. Nevertheless, the chapter begins with some concrete observations, and these are quite telling. In a rare personal disclosure, he recounts a recurrent dream, in which "Uniformed men have blocked the only way out of a tall building and are making arrests, beginning with the lower floor and gradually working their way up to me. Their uniforms are German, or sometimes Russian." The derivation of the dream is quite clear, and he adds that "the dream is usually composed of fragments of streets and houses from my memory." (I wonder if all immigrants have such dreams; when I first returned to Kraków, after a seventeen-year absence, I recognized the turns of its streets and alleyways from my dreams.)

But the real purpose of the dream is to indicate the reasons for his wonder at American democracy, and the idea—so antithetical to authoritarian regimes—that "the power of the state should have limits prescribed by law and that nobody should be thrown in prison on the whim of men in uniform." This, despite declaring that he has no idea how the "American system" works. Mind you, how many immigrants did—or do? I found myself perpetually baffled by the checks and balances, the state laws and the federalism, the dullness of the procedures contrasting with the fervor and even violence of political debates—by the very vastness of American democracy.

It is interesting that Miłosz's views on America are partly formed by the country's contrasts not only with the Other Europe but with the country of his first exile—France. The allusions to his French period in his summing up suggest that his rancor at his treatment there was still alive. "Despite all the years I lived in Western Europe, I did not have even a single offer from any institution concerned with propagating knowledge," he writes. French cultural institutions and its educational system were, in his estimation, conservative to the core and stuck in the nineteenth century. It is also through his (and his sons') experiences in France that he analyzes, with prescient insight, the sources of economic inequality, in terms with which we have become newly familiar recently. Inequality, he notes, begins in childhood, not only with elementary school education but at home, where the children of the more privileged classes absorb a sense of language and the possibilities of self-expression—a basic form of cultural capital—unavailable to those who grow up in less upscale households. In France, he notes, these divisions are reinforced early on in schools, where "children of eleven are classified—some will go to the *lycée,* and are immediately marked for the upper class, and others will prepare for the 'lower' economic occupations." In America, he thought, class divisions persist (as they indeed did, despite the very notion of "class" being a sort of taboo), but the possibilities of advancement, of admission to university and upward mobility, were much better there for people from all backgrounds.

On the whole, Europe was the past—America the future, and in his "Summing Up," Miłosz contemplates the latter both as an inhabitant appreciating its merits and from a distance that seems (and in some ways actually is) interplanetary. His own condition there is easier than it was in Europe, not only because he is employed and appreciated but because, in America, everyone is homeless, uprooted, alienated ("for who besides the Indians was not an alien?"). But his concern in the essay is really the crisis of Western civilization—most evident in America, and especially on its far-flung Pacific coast.

On one, very concrete level, the crisis in his view is caused by the despoliations of nature through technology and by the phantasmagoric amounts of waste the country produces. Above all, the deep civilizational disorientation, in Miłosz's large-scale vision, is propelled by profound changes in the spatial imagination. Beginning with the opening lines of *Visions*—"I am here"—the forms and deformations of space are a motif that runs through all his reflections, and in his summing up, his imagination travels from the concrete sites of American landscapes to the cosmos itself. Ultimately, the crisis of hypermodernity, and that illness difficult to name, follows, in his view, from the loss of a hieratic understanding of space—that is, a cosmos imaginatively structured by the ideas of Heaven, Earth, and Hell, which have permeated art and philosophy for centuries and have allowed humans to make sense of our existential situation. In a universe literally deconstructed by relativity, it is harder to make sense of our condition. This is quite arcane, but in a wonderful illustration of the changes brought about by science, he describes the first images of the earth sent from outer space—and the first messages sent by American astronauts, which, significantly for him, were religious ("In the beginning, God created the heavens and the earth . . ."). Of course, whether one is religious or not, the images of the round earth as seen from a cosmic perspective were stunning—and I think everyone who saw them felt that they portended a paradigm shift in our perceptions as fundamental as the Copernican revolution. For Miłosz, the sight of "our huge, round, blue home" is a cause for wonder and acceptance of our specific place in the universe. "Instead of anger at existence, did we perhaps for a moment feel love for good water, good trees, good plants?" And then his thought leaps further still, to an acceptance—perhaps through that moon-orbiting epiphany—of that loss of hieratic space he had rued before. "Besides," he reflects, "it is not only interplanetary voyages that are imperceptibly reconstructing the imagination, but also the heterogeneity of times; the multiplicity of times; the multiplicity of possible spaces . . . everything science reveals, changing reality from a mechanism into a crystal cabinet of wonders." This is far-seeing enough to be, indeed, visionary, and *Visions from San Francisco Bay* finishes on a note of fundamental amazement: "that something like America exists, and that humanity still exists." And that he is there.

▣ *Visions* was first published in Polish by the Literary Institute in 1969 and then brought out in English in 1975. Miłosz's poetic output that followed was prodigious, and it can be arbitrarily divided between poems of the present moment and poems of the long past. Here's a short poem written in 1971, called "Gift":

A day so happy.
Fog lifted early, I worked in the garden.
Hummingbirds were stopping over
    honeysuckle flowers.
There was no thing on earth I wanted to
    possess.
I knew no one worth my envying him.
Whatever evil I had suffered, I forgot.
To think that once I was the same man did
    not embarrass me.
In my body I felt no pain.
When straightening up, I saw the blue sea
    and sails.

Here we have the gift of simple pleasure, unproblematic and uncomplicated, and perhaps it is not an accident that the poem was written not long after Miłosz finished grappling with the meanings of America. Now he could experience its natural beauty in all its immediacy, without comparisons or an accompanying sense of regret.

Miłosz's capacity for pleasure, his sheer, robust vitality, were evident to all those who knew him and are reflected in much of his late poetry. But many of the poems written from California in the 1970s turn, across those unbridgeable geographical and historical distances, to the vanished past. This is poetry that proceeds from a deep vein of loss and an urgent need to recapture the world which formed him. The urge is both personal and historical, and in many works from this period—most notably the long sequence entitled "From the Rising of the Sun"— Miłosz attempts his task of revival by combining poetic fragments with extended, densely factual prose sections, in which he chronicles fragments of his family past and, to most of his readers, entirely obscure history. I don't think such works were primarily experiments in form; Miłosz disliked the very idea of such endeavors. Rather, it seems to me that the battering intensity of this long, *sui generis* work reflects an almost metaphysical need to do the impossible: to bring back, through some alchemical process, what no longer exists.

"From the Rising of the Sun" is a work of great poignancy. It is clearly an attempt to revive what was lost but also, as Miłosz entered his sixth decade—which to him heralded the onset of old age—to come to terms with his own life. It's worth quoting at length from the beginning sequence of this strange and moving composition. Here's the second verse of "The Rising's" first part, called "The Unveiling":

This time I am frightened. Odious rhythmic speech
Which grooms itself and, of its own accord, moves on.
Even if I wanted to stop it, weak as I am from fever,
Because of a flu like the last one that brought mournful revelations
When, looking at the futility of my ardent years,
I heard a storm from the Pacific beating against the window.
But no, gird up your loins, pretend to be brave to the end
Because of daylight and the neighing of the red horse.

Vast lands. Flickering of hazy trains.
Children walk by an open field, all is gray beyond an Estonian village.

Royza, captain of the cavalry. Mowczan.
    Angry gales.
Never again will I kneel in my small country,
    by a river,
So that what is stone in me could be
    dissolved,
So that nothing would remain but my tears,
    tears.

The poet here is in what seems to be in a half-hallucinatory state—at the mercy of "odious rhythmic speech," which takes over against his will. But he is compelled to remember; he must remember. The conflation of his present state with "a storm from the Pacific beating against the window," and the summons of the inescapable, equally present past conveys a sense of his inner turmoil, of being caught in the storm of memory. There are flickers of what he saw in childhood, as his family traveled through the region of Estonia during World War I, his first glimpses of chaos and destruction. There is the need to be brave as he hears the "neighing of the red horse"—one of the horses of the Apocalypse, usually identified with war. Is the memory of destruction what summons him, yet again, to his poetic duty? He knows, of course, that poetry cannot accomplish literal revival. However much the past lives in him, he cannot return to his "small country, by a river / So that what is stone in me could be dissolved." This is poignant in the extreme, an indirect admission of an impossible longing, and a sensation many exiles know: the hardening of the self against loss, which could become overwhelming if given rein.

"From the Rising of the Sun" contains a Chorus—signaling that we are in a timeless, classical world—passing stern judgment on the poet as it might on Oedipus or Agamemnon:

> He whose life was short can easily be
>   forgiven.
> He whose life was long can hardly be
>   forgiven.
> When will that shore appear from which at
>   last we see
> How all this came to pass and for what
>   reason?

This lifts the poet's individual fate to the level of tragedy and brings in that element of fundamental questioning which drives so much of Miłosz's poetry. The questions can never be answered, of course—unless it is from death's other shore—and the poem ends on a note that comes as close as anything in Miłosz's writing to heartbreak:

> Again the other, unnamed one, speaks for me.
> And he opens fading dream-like houses

So that I write here in desolation
Beyond the land and sea.

The fading dream-like houses are opened and described in great detail in subsequent parts of this long, eccentric work. Is this accomplished by his earlier self? Or by a more arcane force—a ghostly Other within, made more inaccessible by distance in time and space? Whatever drives him, Miłosz returns to the task again and again, through prose and poetry, through fact and contemplation, as in these lines from the sequence "Diary of a Naturalist":

> My generation was lost. Cities too. And
>   nations.
> But all this a little later. Meanwhile, in the
>   window, a swallow
> Performs its rite of the second. That boy,
>   does he already suspect
> That beauty is always elsewhere and always
>   delusive?

Great loss, juxtaposed with a moment of evanescent presence: here are the two polarities driving so much of his poetry, driving him to attempt the impossible again and again.

It must be said that aside from being eerily affecting, "From the Rising of the Sun" is in some ways an obsessional, indeed an almost hallucinatory work. Between passages of poetry it recounts, in long prose passages, the history of the Miłosz family's corner of Lithuania, complete with obscure place-names, dates, and events that would have had no meaning for his American readers—or, for that matter, most of his Polish ones. For example, the third part of the work, "Lauda," contains a disquisition on the meaning of that word, "which is neither an Italian nor a Polish lauda, but is the Lithuanian Liauda and is not related to the Latin laudare. The small river Liaude flows through it and feeds the river Niewiaza on its way to receiving five tributaries: the Nekelpa, the Garduva, the Kemsrotas, the Nykis, and the Viesnanta." There it is again, the primal river, the Heraclitean flow, but rather than invoking the ineffable beauty of nature, "Lauda" goes on to recount in great documentary detail—in archaic Polish—the history of Miłosz's family, including the inventory of its household, the story of a small church in its vicinity, a forgotten insurrection, as well as observations about the high school he attended and comments about the Lithuanian origins of many Polish writers (above all, the great nineteenth-century bard, Mickiewicz), all the while interspersing fragments of poetic autobiography.

It is hard to know for whom—to whom—this work was written, but there is purpose here, however unconcerned with a potential audience. The poem is in part a reckoning with himself, addressed, in a sense, to himself. But it seems to me that above all, he wanted—needed—to assert that his native realm, his small corner of the world, mattered; that it contained interesting personalities and great writers; that—however obscure its history—it was part of the civilized world. It is, after all, one of the characteristics of a developed culture that it keeps records of itself, and in one of his startling leaps between epochs and continents, Miłosz shifts from the obscure chronicles of the "Apytalaukis parish" to the Museum of Modern Art in Berkeley, "to have a look at an exhibition of the projected cities of the future." Here, he encounters models of futuristic gigantism and buildings that could hold a million inhabitants. This doesn't bode well for anyone paying attention to an obscure corner of Lithuania, but in his own prophecy of the future, Miłosz avers that "we should not discount the curiosity of computers, a company of which will reflect on everything—among other obscurities, my origin and descent."

Given that he was writing in the early 1970s, this was indeed prophetic. But in the poetry woven throughout "From the Rising of the Sun," Miłosz stays close to his all-too-human self and travels through his own, internal memory, remembering his childhood and education, his spiritual development—as well as his flaws:

> The young man was cleverly constructed.
> He was inhabited by a vulgar and lunatic ego.
> He demanded love, admiration, the murmurs
>   of praise. . . .
>
> Nevertheless, despite everything or because
>   of it,
> Inside he had nothing but fear.
> Fear of others' eyes, fear of touch, fear of
>   human morals,
> Fear of life greater than fear of death,
> And scornfulness and high fastidiousness.

In the sixth poem of the sequence, "The Accuser," the confession turns into a sort of self-mockery:

> Do you still say to yourself: *non omnis moriar*?
>
> Oh yes, not all of me shall die, there will
>   remain
> An item in the fourteenth volume of an
>   encyclopedia
> Next to a hundred Millers and Mickey
>   Mouse.

From an obscure Lithuanian hamlet to San Francisco Bay, from historical past to the hypertechnological future, from the Bible to pop culture—Miłosz's range was enormous, and his need to grasp it all came close to a kind of torment.

But "From the Rising of the Sun" also moves at several points from inner conflict to reconciliation, from the anguish of his inadequacy to acceptance:

—Yet I have learned how to live with my grief.

—As if putting words together has been of help.

—Not true, there were others, grace and beauty.

I bowed to them, revered them,
I brought them my gifts.

—And all you do is repeat:
If only there were enough time.
If only there were enough time.

There never is, of course, and hence, perhaps, the urgent need to remember and record—and to create. The underlying urge of this eccentric and in some ways anguished work is suggested in its last part, "Bells in Winter." There, Miłosz returns to a very ordinary memory of a room he rented in Vilnius and an "old servant woman, Lisabeth":

> There is, it would seem, no reason
> (For I have departed to a land more distant
> Than one that can be reached by roads
>   leading through woods and mountains)
> To bring that room back here.
>
> Yet I belong to those who believe in
>   *apokatastasis.*
> The word promises reverse movement. . . .
>
> It means: restoration. So believed: St
>   Gregory of Nyssa,
> Johannes Scotus Erigena, Ruysbroeck, and
>   William Blake.
>
> For me, therefore, everything has a double
>   existence.
> Both in time and when time shall be no more.

Time lost and time recaptured. Worlds lost and worlds recaptured. For Miłosz, in his travels across both, Mnemosyne, the main goddess of his later years, offers the hope (which for him had Christian and mystical connotations) of acceptance and metaphoric restoration.

Mnemosyne has been the muse of many exiles, and much wonderful literature has emerged from following its bidding: Nabokov's *Speak,*

Memory, Brodsky's "In a Room and a Half," the lovely recently rediscovered essays by the Polish-Jewish writer Joseph Wittlin, Nadezhda Mandelstam's magisterial *Hope against Hope*, as well as works by Milan Kundera, Josef Škvorecký, and many others.

But it must be said that during his Berkeley years, from the far distances of the Pacific shore, Miłosz's turn to memory sometimes takes on the qualities of a compulsion. Perhaps his consciousness of the distances from which he was writing—both spatial and temporal—intensified his anguished need to bridge both. In a long work called *The Separate Notebooks*, he once again combines fragments of poetry and prose in an attempt to remember and record—everything. Everything. Errant details and family chronicles, stories of ghosts haunting a Lithuanian castle, the markings on his father's uniform, the years of independence in Poland, and—above all—the many lost, individual people for whom his memory is the only guarantee of being remembered; really, of having existed.

This, of course, continues to be one reason for the strength of Miłosz's preoccupation: the need to commemorate the dead, especially those who died tragically and needlessly in the ravages of World War II, and through those acts of gratuitous violence that have come to be known as the Holocaust. It is as if Miłosz is fulfilling his own prophecy in "A Poor Christian Looks at the Ghetto" and, like the guardian mole, sorting out the ashes of the dead, and identifying them in all their particularity. There is a long section in *Separate Notebooks* addressed to Cézanne, about a painter named Mieczysław, who might have "snatched from things a moment of seeing / had he observed the rules of the artist / who must be indifferent to good and evil." But instead, "he used his workshop to help people / and hid Jews there, for which the penalty was death / He was executed in May 1943 / thus giving his soul for his friends." Miłosz follows this with a prose vignette of Mieczysław and his wife and friends, enjoying bohemian company and mountaineering before the war. The juxtaposition is heartbreaking, but the sequence ends on a note of something like metaphysical consolation: "He thinks that the word *past* does not mean anything, for if he can keep those three so strongly before his eyes, how much stronger than his is an unearthly gaze."

After such knowledge, what forgiveness. The imperative to remember, the need to break through words to the vanished reality itself— literally, to revive—is for Miłosz not only personal but powerfully ethical. "How to speak? How to tear apart the skin of words? / What I have written seems to me now not that. / And what I have lived seems to me now not that."

◈ The magnetic pull of a tragic past is powerful. But some of the poems written in the later 1970s begin to sound notes of more serene acceptance. Perhaps there was a sense of duty fulfilled? Miłosz had surely done all he could—almost more than might seem possible—to strive against forgetting. Now, perhaps, he was freed to turn to the present, as in a poem called "A Portal":

> Before a sculpted stone portal,
> In the sun, at the border of light and shade,
> Almost serene. Thinking with relief: this
>   will remain
> When the frail body fades and presto,
>   nobody.

Something will remain, even when he is no longer there to carry the vanished world in his memory.

In a later sequence, "After Paradise," memory is not abandoned, but the note of reconciliation to the present begins to sound more often. Interestingly, his poems from this time also become more directly personal, and sometimes erotic. The presence of women was always threaded through Miłosz's writings, but in "After Paradise," it is often accompanied by the language of sexuality and desire.

> Don't run anymore. Quiet. How softly it rains
> On the roofs of the city. How perfect
> All things are. Now, for the two of you
> Waking up in a royal bed by a garret window.
> For a man and a woman. For one plant
> divided
> Into masculine and feminine which longed
> for each other.

This is Platonic, in its suggestion of an original androgyny, from which sexual longing proceeds. But there are more explicit passages as well: "I liked your velvet yoni, Annalena, long voyages in the delta of your legs." It is startling to read this in a Miłosz poem—especially one written at a later age—but it is as if the hidden subtext of his potent pansexuality now turns more explicitly to human sexuality, and the metaphysics of time and loss, of history and movement, are now supplanted, or at least supplemented, by the pleasure and fullness of living human presence, which is, often enough, feminine and erotic. Sometimes this is combined with the urges and urgency of memory, as in this ending of a prose sequence called "The Hooks of a Corset": "Her flesh which has turned to dust is as desirable to me as it was to that other man and if I touch her in my dream she does not even mention that she has died long ago. On the verge of a great discovery I almost penetrate the secret of the Particular transforming itself into the General and of the General transforming itself into the Particular. I endow with a philosophical meaning the moment when I helped her to undo the hooks of her corset." In this passage, memory of an erotic moment is recovered in a dream, and death is in a sense vanquished by the exactitude of remembrance. But the feminine presence is now also depicted in three dimensions, through allusions to actual liaisons in the past, adventitious encounters, details of women's clothes and their gestures. Miłosz's memory was, as ever, precise.

Possibly, there were some quite private reasons for this unexpected turn to eroticism and intimate disclosure. Miłosz's first wife, Janina, who was by all accounts a very attractive as well as a highly intelligent and charming person, fell tragically ill in the mid-1970s, and after being misdiagnosed with ALS while suffering from cancer of the spine, she was bedbound and used a wheelchair. When I interviewed Miłosz, a young and attractive woman was present at the conversation and periodically left the room to check on Janina. Miłosz explained to me what was happening. Clearly, the arrangement was known and accepted by all.

At the same time (to be entirely speculative for a moment), I wonder if, believing that he had reached old age, Miłosz felt reprieved from the reproach of lawless sexuality. But perhaps the turn to the present, and to freer personal disclosure, also had something to do with the altered political situation in Poland, and the possibility of returning there not only through memory and language but in reality. Quite possibly, the award of the Nobel Prize in 1980 to a previously unknown writer also had to do with that new situation, and the rise of the movement known as Solidarity. The Nobel is known to be driven by political as well as purely literary considerations, and the eyes of the world were, in that dramatic moment, turned toward Poland and the heroic behavior of the workers who drove the demands for a change of regime and for freedom. The previously obscure country behind the Iron Curtain suddenly mattered, and Miłosz was its worthy and inspiring voice. Of course, Miłosz fully deserved the honor on purely literary grounds, and, possibly, his work was at least for some members of the Swedish Academy a great discovery.

After he was awarded the Nobel, Miłosz was able to visit Poland for the first time since his defection in 1951—following a nearly thirty-year severance!—and was given a hero's welcome. He met Lech Wałęsa and Pope John Paul II. Eventually, words from his poem "You Who Wronged" were inscribed on the memorial to the fallen shipyard workers in Gdańsk, where the Solidarity movement started and heroically continued against great odds. Here, the words of the poem acquired a newly powerful meaning:

> You who wronged a simple man . . .
> . . . Do not feel safe. The poet remembers.
> You can kill one, but another is born.
> The words are written down, the deed, the
>   date.

Given his respect for the "simple man" and for work, I think Miłosz would have been greatly moved by this. At the same time, his books were officially published in Poland for the first time since 1951, and this would surely have been not only important but reparative: a healing of a rupture that was also a wound. I had a glimpse of what publication in his native realm meant to Miłosz when I happened to talk to him shortly after his poetry was published, for the first time ever, in Lithuanian. He was as thrilled as if it were his very first publication altogether. I remember feeling rather amazed by his almost youthful excitement and the strength of attachment it suggested—as well as a kind of modesty. He could still feel excited at being published!

He was also moved to discover that, despite being censored, his poetry was known in Poland, especially among the young. Throughout his émigré decades, he continued to publish essays and poetry with the *Kultura* press in Paris, and from the later 1960s on, these began reaching (via smuggled publications) a select group of readers in Poland itself—and students involved in protest movements began quoting some of his verses as a sort of political catechism.

His reaction to receiving the Nobel itself was wonderfully unpretentious. On the day when he was notified of this honor—the highest, after all, a living writer can receive—he went right back to the classroom. He had tried to retire earlier, but in order to be able to pay for Janina's treatment, he continued to teach seminars in Slavic literature. He was not, however, unaware of the distinction being bestowed upon him. In the so-called Banquet Speech given on the day of the award, he noted that although he taught at a university that had many Nobelists to its name, he was pleased to be the first one to be awarded the prize in the humanities. No excessive pride—and no false modesty. After returning to Berkeley, he refused to park his car in a special lot reserved for those fellow Nobelists, mostly awarded for their work in economics and science. Parking spaces at Berkeley were worth their weight in gold, but Miłosz apparently didn't want to draw on such special privileges. Perhaps he wished, even then, to remain one working person among others.

In his main acceptance speech at the Nobel ceremony itself, Miłosz sounded many of the notes familiar from his writings—and some that seemed additionally revealing. He said (and this was clearly not only courtesy to his Swedish hosts) that during his school years, he read *The Library of the Nobel Laureates*, and that among them, *The Wonderful Adventures of Nils*, by Selma Lagerlöf, a Swedish Nobelist, was a particular influence, because its hero "flies above the Earth and looks at it from above but at the same time sees it in every detail"—an image that so presciently forecasts his own, mature mode of vision. Indeed, one need look no further than this moving and meaning-filled speech to understand the sources and the catalysts of Miłosz's poetry. He spoke of the poetic endeavor as a quest for reality, or *esse*—a serious and ethical task, which he counterposed to various notions of formal experiments or theories of *écriture*, then modish in academia and intellectual circles. Indeed, he stressed that he thought of himself not as an inspired individual "artist" but as a voice representing an underestimated literary tradition and emerging from that insufficiently understood Other Europe—a part of the world "marked by enormous disasters" but which also, he noted, possessed certain advantages: "It is good to be born in a small country where Nature was on a human scale, where various languages and religions cohabited for centuries."

Even as he was achieving international fame, Miłosz was not going to abandon his first attachments, but he also mentioned Simone Weil, a Jewish mystical philosopher who converted to Catholicism and was one of his spiritual exemplars. "Distance is the soul of beauty," she said, and distance, movement across the many kinds of spaces he traveled in reality and in his writing, was something he experienced on every level of emotion and thought. But he also admitted that in the face of history such as that which ravaged his native realm, the distance of internal detachment (that distance which, in the midst of horror, he had tried so hard to achieve) was impossible to maintain. He also spoke about the phenomenon among the younger generations of Holocaust denial—genuinely distressing for someone like him, who felt a continuing obligation to those who died during that genocide. And, with his usual striving for full truthfulness, he alluded to a different kind of forgetfulness, of the many non-Jewish groups—the millions of Poles, Russians, Ukrainians and people of other nationalities—who suffered and died during World War II.

Memory, in Miłosz's Nobel presentation, and less explicitly in his poetry, is an instrument and aspect of morality, and collective memory in his native realm (where "The War" was still part of intergenerational consciousness) is contrasted with the great forgetfulness in other parts of the world—a widespread amnesia that, he felt, was enabled in part by the proliferation of digital technologies. As usual, his perceptions moved between history and the cutting edge of the present; and in thinking about both, the question of the Other Europe, and all the misunderstandings he had seen and experienced in relation to it, were clearly still alive for him and still rankling.

Shortly after the Nobel ceremonies, Miłosz stopped briefly in Paris, where he met for an interview with a prewar friend, Jerzy Turowicz—the founder and editor of a dissident Catholic weekly published in Kraków, which was among the first to write about the continuing problems of Polish anti-Semitism. (The journal's publication was continuous in the postwar period, except for three years in the 1950s, when Turowicz refused to write an ode to Stalin after his death.) I don't know how long it had been since the two met, but the transcript of their conversation (conducted in Polish) has the immediacy and intimacy that proceed from their long friendship—as well as a shared, lived knowledge of Poland's history. "Czesławie," Turowicz begins, addressing Miłosz intimately, and not without a hint of affectionate irony, "the Nobel Prize has fashioned you into a prophet. How do you feel in this role?" "Not quite," Miłosz answers, in another bit of untranslatable self-deprecation. "I used to write for a small number of people, and now suddenly this changed. Quality into quantity. Yes?" "A change in the opposite direction than according to the laws of dialectical materialism," Turowicz responds. This exchange draws on a long and close acquaintance with each other's turns of thought, and so does their discussion of Miłosz's translations of the Bible. Miłosz talks about the relative difficulties of translating the Old Testament from Hebrew and Greek (the latter is easier!) and, with touching directness explains that this task not only has a particular importance for him but was helpful when he was visiting his ill wife in the hospital every day. Translation is "philological work" that requires a "workshop," and this was steadying. But it also requires a certain self-effacement, which, in the unsettling circumstances, was "stabilizing." Work—especially modest or even self-effacing work—was, as ever, the saving grace.

Conversations such as the one with Turowicz must have been reparative: a kind of knitting together of the past and present. But Miłosz was also impressed by the young people he met in Poland: by their "acuteness" of mind and their knowledge of wartime history, which was still, in that generation, fully alive—as it was not among his American students or, for that matter, among Polish immigrants in America. He was also touchingly pleased to meet quite a few Polish exiles in Sweden who were acquainted with his work (presumably via *Kultura*'s publications). These were almost certainly Polish Jews who felt they could no longer remain in Poland after 1968, when the Communist Party took a virulently anti-Semitic turn.

"Perhaps the only memory," Miłosz said in his Nobel speech, "is the memory of wounds," and much of his most powerful poetry sprang from its imperatives. But during his long years of exile, Miłosz remained faithful to his past in other ways. Translation may have been a steadying occupation, as he told Turowicz—but it was also an expression of a deep attachment and a mission. However strongly he rebelled against the politics of both pre- and postwar Poland, he loved—and was devoted to—Polish literature, and he clearly considered it part of his task to make it better known in the wider world.

Aside from his own writing, he conceived a project that continues to be important to this day—an English-language anthology titled *Postwar Polish Poetry*, first published in 1965, which for many non-Polish readers was their first introduction to Miłosz's own poetry as well as to such eminent Polish poets as Zbigniew Herbert, Tadeusz Różewicz, and the future Nobel Prize winner Wisława Szymborska. The anthology was a revelation not only to the "common reader" but to many English-language poets, for whom Polish literature had been a *terra incognita*. Miłosz's translations of his own poetry and those of his fellow Poles introduced possibilities of thematic range and sheer seriousness that for some American literati were quite revelatory. This was not art for art's sake, art as an experiment, art as an expression of alienation, or art as a decorative add-on; rather, Polish poetry was most often a response to tragic historical realities and a quest for hard-won truths—however ironically, in some cases, these were expressed. W. S. Merwin wrote that "Miłosz's book had been a talisman and had made most of the literary bickering among the various ideological encampments, then most audible in the poetic doctrines in English, seem frivolous and silly." Seamus Heaney called Miłosz a "sage and acknowledged master," and the friendship between the two poets—two future Nobel Prize winners—was important for them both. One wonders if part of their affinity sprang from their shared origins in the provinces of larger empires, which in both cases saw more than their share of collective violence but also created more than their proportion of great literature. And there were other poets for whom Miłosz, once he became known, was a discovery and a lodestar: Joseph Brodsky, Robert Pinsky, Derek Walcott, and yet more.

Miłosz translated others, and he owed much to being translated. I doubt that he would have been considered for the Nobel had his work existed only in Polish. Still, I wonder how he felt about reading himself in English (or other languages). He had devoted and wonderful translators, some of whom he met at Berkeley, and he spoke and wrote about them with gratitude; he said there were often good times and laughter as they labored over transporting his poems into English together.

Miłosz's poetry in English is rich and resonant, but the act of translation—surely, most of all for a poet—almost inevitably includes an element of loss. "What is lost in translation is the poetry," Robert Frost declared. That is perhaps too pessimistic, but the distance between Polish and English is quite vast—yet another kind of internal distance that Miłosz had to traverse. The soundscape, the music of Polish is very different from English. Polish is not a euphonious language like, say, Russian or French, but it has a forceful expressiveness and a complex grammar, which compels logical construction more strongly, and lends itself to rhyme more easily, than is true in English. And for all his love of other literatures—English poetry in particular—it was Polish that was part of Miłosz's body and mind. If he were a writer who cultivated aesthetic detachment or "the alienation effect," he might have wanted to shift to writing in his second language, as, for example, Samuel Beckett did; but that was not a poetic attitude he valued. He wanted his poetry to come as close to Being as possible.

In his banquet speech, Miłosz spoke about Polish literature, "which is relatively little known in the world as it is hardly translatable. Comparing it with other literatures, I have been able to appreciate its rich oddity. It is a kind of secret brotherhood with its own rites of communion with the dead, where weeping and laughter, pathos and irony coexist on an equal footing, history-oriented, always allusive[;] in this century, as before, it faithfully accompanied the people in their hard trials. Lines of Polish verse circulated underground, were written in barracks of concentration camps and in soldiers' tents in Asia, Africa, and Europe."

This is moving and true—as I discovered when I did a radio program on poetry written in the Warsaw Ghetto. "It was the most real thing we had," one of its survivors told me—a tribute to the power of poetry that surely cannot be bettered. Of course, there are other nations with rich, history-informed and history-scarred literatures. But at the time Miłosz paid his tribute to his native tongue, Polish, in addition to its intrinsic difficulties, was thought of as a culturally "minor" language, and his defense of it undoubtedly sprang in part from that awareness. The question of the Other Europe has many dimensions, and the sense that their country's literary wealth remained unrecognized was felt acutely by Polish poets and intellectuals.

I am not a poet, nor was ever destined to become one, but in my first years of school, I was brought up on Polish literature, which includes some classic works—preeminently the great nineteenth-century epic, *Pan Tadeusz*, by Miłosz's fellow Lithuanian, Adam Mickiewicz—written in Parisian exile. This re-creation of a lost world is as much a novel in verse as it is an epic poem, and I remember the first enchantment of hearing / reading / reciting its verses when I attended school in Kraków in the 1950s. A beautiful edition of *Pan Tadeusz*, with fold-out watercolor illustrations, is one of the few books that, during my family's own, difficult emigration, made it across to Canada, and which I've taken with me to wherever I have subsequently lived.

I was young enough to make English my primary, if not chronologically first language. But I still feel a pang of regret at the near impossibility of conveying the beauty, the drama, and the wonderfully light comedy of *Pan Tadeusz* to my English-speaking friends. The first language lives a long and mysterious life within one's psyche and mind—and so, perhaps, do attachments to one's first culture. I confess it was a special satisfaction for me to see the work of Polish poets reviewed in the *New York Times* in the 1980s and to see discussions of Polish poets—Zbigniew Herbert, Adam Zagajewski, Wisława Szymborska, and Anna Swir, among others—being effortlessly included in programs on poetry in New York and London as well as in other parts of Europe. Miłosz's own labors contributed to this new awareness greatly, as did the international recognition of his own poetry and its exemplary power for other poets.

By the time I met Miłosz in 1981, the situation in Poland—such was the speed of events—had changed again, as the workers' rebellion was crushed and martial law imposed. I think Miłosz felt this as an almost personal blow and talked about his own dashed hopes for Poland. But I imagine that his first, temporary return—before his later, more permanent one—would have been reparative, a symbolic healing of a painful (if bravely accepted) split. His two worlds, so far apart until then, were coming closer together. Perhaps this meant that he didn't have to keep reimagining the past quite so compulsively in order to revive it; the past now existed to some extent within the present and was remembered by others as well—as in his moving poem "Caffé Greco," written in Rome in 1986, in which he meets again with Jerzy Turowicz:

> In the eighties of the twentieth century, in
>   Rome, via Condotti
> We were sitting with Turowicz in the Caffé
>   Greco
> And I spoke in, more or less, these words:
>
> —We have seen much, comprehended much.
> States were falling, countries passed away . . .
>
> By what can literature redeem itself
> If not by a melopoeia of praise, a hymn
> Even unintended? And you have my
>   admiration,

> For you accomplished more than did my
> companions
> Who once sat here, the proud geniuses.
> . . . With age and with the waning of this age
> One learns to value wisdom, and simple
> goodness.

A shared past, and a shared understanding, in which a complex and dark history resolves itself into the simplicity of acceptance—and friendship. In "Caffé Greco," the two friends are meeting in Rome rather than Poland, but the possibility of such encounters might have lightened Miłosz's burden of remembrance and its obligations. Perhaps he felt, after that first return to Poland, that he no longer had to carry the past—"the memory of wounds"—all by himself: that he was now entitled to living as one person among others, not forgetting—he never did—but unburdened enough to turn to the possibilities and pleasures of the present.

"A Confession," written in 1985, is an acknowledgment of something that was evident in Miłosz's personality to all who knew him but rarely entered his earlier poetry: a kind of ordinary, sensuous, fully human appetite for life:

> My Lord, I loved strawberry jam
> And the dark sweetness of a woman's body.

Also well-chilled vodka, herring in olive oil,
Scents, of cinnamon, of cloves.
So what kind of prophet am I? Why should
    the spirit
Have visited such a man? Many others
Were justly called, and trustworthy.
Who would have trusted me? For they saw
How I empty glasses, throw myself on food,
And glance greedily at the waitress's neck.

The poem ends on a note of self-deprecation, but his self-criticism is now simple and simply human; he is not guilty of failing to save nations, or of betraying the spirit of history, or of not being able to penetrate the mysteries of the cosmos. He is guilty of being an ordinary, flawed, sensuous man.

Miłosz's wife, Janina, died in 1986, after a long period of terrible illness; a poem called "On Parting with My Wife, Janina" contains metaphors of fire that suggest the sense of her terrible suffering, as her body was consumed by illness, but it also expresses an all-too-human sense of guilt and loss:

I loved her, without knowing who she really
    was.
I inflicted pain on her, chasing my illusion.
I betrayed her with women, though faithful
    to her only.

> We lived through much happiness and
>   unhappiness,
> Separations, miraculous rescues. And now,
>   this ash.
> And the sea battering the shore when I walk
>   the empty boulevard.
> And the sea battering the shore. And
>   ordinary sorrow.

"Ordinary sorrow" rather than transpersonal, all-consuming guilt and anguish. The repetition of "the sea battering the shore" has a vast melancholy; undoubtedly, the sorrow was deep. But it came after a death that was part of the ordinary human condition rather than of collective horror, and combined with the simple confessional lines of the poem this, also, is a note that, even in the midst of mourning, suggests a kind of acceptance.

One might have also thought that receiving the Nobel would have led Miłosz to let up on his practically Stakhanovite rate of production. But writing was apparently as necessary to him as breathing, and he continued to work as he ever did, exploring some of his fundamental themes in new ways. And, however self-deprecating he could be sometimes about the profession of poetry or his own importance, I think he was consoled by the new assurance that his work would not be forgotten. These are a few lines from a poem called "And Yet the Books," written in 1986:

> And yet the books will be there on the
>   shelves, separate beings . . .
> . . . So much more durable
> Than we are, whose frail warmth
> Cools down with memory, disperses,
>   perishes.
> I imagine the earth when I am no more:
> Nothing happens, no loss, it's still a strange
>   pageant,
> Women's dresses, dewy lilacs, a song in the
>   valley.
> Yet the books will be there on the shelves,
>   well born,
> Derived from people, but also from radiance,
>   heights.

Acceptance of mortality, aided by the thought of his books lasting beyond his death, surely also accounted for the new notes in his poetry. These are quite discernible in the poems written after the "Changes" of 1989, when travel to eastern Europe became once again possible—and when Miłosz began to move back quite regularly between Berkeley and Kraków. His personal fate was, as ever, linked to the larger movements of history, and I think this late turn of the wheel may have also led, paradoxically, to a more vivid immersion in the here and now—as in the short poem "In Common," written in 1991:

What is good? Garlic. A leg of lamb on a spit.
Wine with a view of boats rocking in a cove.
A starry sky in August. A rest on a
    mountain peak.

What is good? After a long drive water in a
    pool and a sauna.
Lovemaking and falling asleep, embraced,
    your legs touching hers.
Mist in the morning, translucent,
    announcing a sunny day.

I am submerged in everything that is
    common to us, the living.
Experiencing this earth for them, in my flesh.
Walking past the vague outline of
    skyscrapers? anti-temples?
In valleys of beautiful, though poisoned,
    rivers.

Even more surprising is "Conversations with Jeanne," a longer poem written in the same year and addressed to Jeanne Hersch, a rather severe Swiss philosopher of Polish-Jewish origin with whom Miłosz apparently had a romantic liaison:

Let us not talk philosophy, drop it, Jeanne.
So many words, so much paper, who can
    stand it.
I told you the truth about my distancing
    myself.
I've stopped worrying about my misshapen
    life.
It was no better and no worse than the
    usual human tragedies.

. . . You are right, Jeanne, I don't know how
    to care about the salvation
of my soul.
. . . I accept it, what has befallen me is just.
I don't pretend to the dignity of a wise old
    age.
Untranslatable into words, I chose my home
    in what is now,
In things of this world, which exist and, for
    that reason, delight us:
Nakedness of women on the beach,
    coppery cones of their breasts,
Hibiscus, allamanda, a red lily, devouring
With my eyes, lips, tongue . . .

Miłosz as someone opposed to all this thinking,
all these words? That is new, and so are the notes
of pure, uncomplicated pleasure in things as they
are—a pansexuality that now includes human
sexuality, as if that also were part of the natural

world and is now affirmed without his former anguish or restless questioning. He isn't caught in Zeno's paradox here, isn't trying to approach a reality that remains always out of reach; he is simply within it.

❋ Miłosz's life, however, continued to be affected by larger events. In 1991, after Lithuania broke away from the Soviet Union, he revisited his country of birth for the first time in seven decades. It was only then that he wrote the essay titled "Happiness," in which he describes not only the childhood state of "perfect happiness" but his later fate, which includes the interventions of history, with its catastrophes and mass death—and, eventually, a change of his own internal state, which at some point altered "from happiness to habitual inner torment." Nevertheless, Miłosz writes, "Happiness experienced in childhood does not pass without a trace." How many exiled writers would confirm this? Nabokov above all, but also many others. Of course, the traces and pathways of that happiness are present in Miłosz's poems of beauty and wonder, scattered throughout a life that contained so much hardship. (When I was writing my memoir, *Lost in Translation*, I wanted to append a section about my Kraków childhood, titled "Paradise," precisely to acknowledge the element of utter, intense happiness before turning to the problematics of emigration. If one is lucky, "the trace" continues to travel through the psyche, whatever the vicissitudes of external events.)

"Happiness" goes on to summarize the intervening history, the despoliations of Miłosz's Edenic landscape and the erasure of whole villages in the name of collectivization. And yet, and yet: "What was most important at the moment was the tangible element of flowing time. I went down to my river." This, almost magically, unlocks the flow within: "Much was going on inside me, and I was stunned by the strength of that current for which no name seemed adequate. It was like waking up from a long dream and becoming again the person whom I have never ceased to be. . . . I was recovering my continuity from myself as a child to myself as an old man." This is moving and powerful: an epiphany that perhaps all of us, but especially those whose lives have held exile and disruption, would wish for. He has been one person, alive through time— and time now flows within him, dissolving that "stone" which his heart had become during a time of unbearable sorrow.

And further: "I was looking at a meadow: Suddenly the realization came that during my years of wandering, I had searched in vain for a combination of leaves and flowers as was here. . . . I understood this after a huge wave of emotion had overwhelmed me, and the only name I can give it now would be—bliss."

The river and the meadow: is this after all the Platonic Real, the thing-in-itself he has kept approaching, and never quite attaining, in his restless quest? Is this the source of his pansexuality, that urgent desire to be so close to the world as to become it? Rivers, with their ceaseless movement, flow through his poetry—the archetype of that Movement which he analyzed in its many guises. And perhaps his conviction that the imagination was spatial derived from that childhood sense of oneness with the bucolic spaces of his childhood.

Certainly, the essay carries a rare cargo, not only of metaphysical questions, but of simple, revelatory emotion; and perhaps the return to the point of origin, the unexpected reconnection with the possibility—and the overwhelming sensation—of simple happiness, accounted for Miłosz's new willingness, in what was now really old age, to give himself over to living in the present. There was also, perhaps both as cause and effect, the unexpected event of his second marriage, in 1992, to Carol Thigpen, an academic at

Emory University. She was thirty-three years younger than him, from the American South, and a writer on radical theories of education. It seemed an unlikely match, but from all evidence, it was based on genuine affection, and it undoubtedly reinforced Miłosz's sense of joie de vivre. Something of the quality of their relationship is conveyed in a poem called "Translating Anna Swir on an Island of the Caribbean":

> By banana plants, on a deck chair, by the
>   pool
> Where Carol, naked, swims her laps
> Of the crawl and the classical style, I
>   interrupt her
> Asking for a synonym. And again I am
>   submerged
> In the murmuring Polish, in meditation.

There are actually two women in the poem: Carol, swimming so startlingly naked as Miłosz is working nearby; and Anna Swir, whose poetry he is translating, and about whom he writes, "When I saw you for the last time / I understood why they liked neither you / Nor your poetry. With that white mane of yours / You could ride a broom, have a devil for a lover."

Swir in his poem is not likable, but she is powerful. Her poetry often speaks of female sen-

suality, but it also has a philosophical thrust—
that search for essential principles which Miłosz
valued. Born in 1909, she died in 1984 and experienced the same historical vicissitudes that
governed Miłosz's life. Being submerged in "the
murmuring Polish" of her poetry, he must have
felt a particular closeness to her, and she is one
of many women who appear, or reappear, in his
late poems. Some are poets whom he met when
he and Carol began to travel quite regularly
between Berkeley and Kraków. Others are fig-
ments of memory, who visit him in dreams or
recollection, returning from his childhood landscapes or from his youth, as if fully, carnally
alive. In many of the poems, he now speaks of
his erotic feelings toward them, often in an uncanny juxtaposition with the knowledge of their
death. In a prose reflection called "Kazia," or in
the poem "Classmate," he tries to reconstruct
the possible fates of a girl and young woman
whom he barely knew, but who keep reappear-
ing in his mind and dreams.

> Does the dream mean I desired her
> Or just felt pity for her former body?

> So that it falls to me to count her scattered
>   bones
> Since I am the last from among that gang of
>   youths from a century past?

A descent into a Dantesque dark hollow
Somewhere near Archangel or in
Kazakhstan?

The dreams, the fragments of the past, never quite let up, but he ends the poem on a note of acceptance.

Farewell, Piorewiczowna, unasked-for
shadow.
I don't even remember your first name.

Perhaps he doesn't have to keep descending into a "Dantesque dark hollow"; perhaps it's all right to let go.

In a quirky, surreal Polish theater piece called "Waltz with Miłosz," Miłosz talks lightly but seriously about himself (in an untranslatable Polish construction) as a kind of feminine-feminist, and however complicated his personal life may have been, I think there are grounds for that self-description. His relationship with Jeanne Hersch, for example, was one of undoubted intellectual equality, and after his gentle rebuke to her, he wrote a long prose poem called "What I Learned from Jeanne Hersch," structured, à la Wittgenstein, like a series of propositions or theses. On another level, *Native Realm* includes portraits of wonderfully competent women keeping Polish prewar institutions from breaking down, and heroic women—including a nun who saved him and his wife from being taken to a concentration camp at the end of the war.

Miłosz's actual returns to the country where he was young, and where so many of those he knew were no longer alive or remembered, may have reinforced not only a sense of acceptance but also, in a different vein, the vividness of memory. The shades of those he knew were closer now, and they seem to rise up from within, almost without his volition, as in these lines from a poem of return, "City of My Youth":

> . . . There was no one left
> Of those who once walked these streets.
> And now they had nothing, except his
>   eyes. . . .
>   . . . His heart was beating,
> Surprising him with its beating, in his body
> Their blood flowed, his arteries fed them
>   with oxygen.
> He felt, inside, their livers, spleens, intestines.
> Masculinity and femininity, elapsed, met in
>   him
> And every shame, every grief, every love.

It is as if he is now not so much a designated mourner as a vehicle, a kind of medium for the shades of both men and women. Their lives exist equally within him, inhabiting him with both masculinity and femininity.

Possibly, this entirely nonideological feminism also had cultural underpinnings. Women were not only active participants in the Warsaw Uprising but in the long history of uprisings, rebellions, and insurrections that marked Polish history. This, of course, continued in the postwar underground and in Solidarity, which had many prominent women leaders. Women went on the lam and into hiding, spent time in prison, and were comrades in arms in the fight for democracy. Not that Polish culture is ideologically feminist—far from it—but whatever political problems women have faced, or are once again facing, the notions of passive, ornamental femininity, of the "silent woman" or of female weakness, were hardly comprehensible to the actual women I met and came to know in Poland.

In the 1990s Miłosz, sometimes accompanied by Carol, moved fairly regularly between Berkeley and Kraków—and other parts of Europe as well. He was now much in demand, all over the world, and his energy was apparently undiminished. In 1993 the couple moved to Kraków permanently, living in various quarters, until an honorary citizenship and a modest apartment was given to them by the city. Miłosz liked Kraków in part because it reminded him of Vilnius. It, too, is a city of churches and synagogues, of baroque and Renaissance architecture, of cobblestoned streets and many cafés. Some of his old friends, including Jerzy Turowicz, still lived there, and there were also younger poets, including Wisława Szymborska, who won the Nobel in 1996, and many others. (As it happens, I was in Kraków in 1996 when, rather amazingly, three Nobelists were present in the city: Miłosz, Szymborska, and Seamus Heaney, whom I had the honor and pleasure to know, and who was a great admirer and friend of Miłosz—as well as a wonderfully insightful commentator on the Polish poet's work. It was a heady day, and I felt that the cultural status of Kraków was fully vindicated. I, too, can occasionally still feel defensive—or proud—on behalf of my native realm.)

Miłosz's late years in Kraków coincided with Poland's post-1989 liberal interregnum—a period during which he could be a truly national figure, celebrated by the old and young, the literati, and even former apparatchiks. But he was also a local hero, someone who was known and loved not only by the literary intelligentsia but by ordinary people. His son Anthony remembers that some of the women who sell flowers in the Rynek—Kraków's great Renaissance square—handed him bouquets of flowers and sometimes embraced him as he walked in that beautiful space or sat in one of the nearby cafés, reading. I imagine this was especially touching to him. After all, it was the ordinary person whom he prized most, and perhaps the vendors who handed him those bouquets understood that, or at least intuited it.

Even now, it gives me great pleasure to think of him in that beautiful square, which is one of my own cherished memory spots, spending leisurely time in one of the many cafés that, even in the impoverished postwar period, hosted so many artists and writers and were the site of so much intimate, energetic, engaged conversation—really, of a specific, central European café culture. I imagine Miłosz must have met there with old and new friends, some of whom, like Adam Zagajewski, belonged to a younger generation of poets, and who not only admired Miłosz but felt directly indebted to him for his influence.

There were other journeys out of exile, and fruitful meetings with younger generations. In 1989 Miłosz visited the town of Sejny, which was part of Lithuania before the war but was now located in Poland, in that land of shifting borders and national identities. While there, he met two young people—Krzysztof Czyżewski and his wife, Małgorzata—who wanted to start a center for the study of multiculturalism in what had been a region of mixed populations, before they were divided by borders or eliminated by war into ethnic homogeneity. This was, of course, an idea that had considerable resonance for Miłosz, and even at his advanced age he was ready to help the Czyżewskis in shaping the project. The Borderland Foundation, which emerged from their conversations, went on to become an internationally recognized center, hosting conferences on various aspects of multiculturalism and doing imaginative, hands-on "memory work" to educate young people in their multicultural past and in the ethics of living with "others." Eventually, Miłosz and his brother Andrzej donated a family-owned manor house near Sejny to the foundation; some two decades later, I found it affecting to take part in a lively conference in that modest but meaning-filled house, attended by guests from various countries. This was clearly work that mattered and continues to do so today, and I think Miłosz would have felt that although not carved in stone, the foundation is also a fitting monument to his life and thought.

Miłosz returned to Poland after a long absence. But for those who stayed, the costs of cooperating with Communist authorities continued to be exacted even after the Velvet Revolutions, when the crimes and misdemeanors committed during the dark years were exposed in newly opened archives and were sometimes punished in an attempt (however flawed) to right the injustices of the past.

The story illustrating this that touched me most closely concerns a prominent translator of English literature into Polish, whom I met in New York in the late 1980s—and who eventually translated three of my own books. Eventually, I met his wife, who was also a writer and a prominent member of a subversive underground cabaret in Kraków—a well-known cultural institution typical of Poland's daring oppositional culture, which continued to provide light entertainment and sharp satire through the censorious years. In 1990 I visited them in their beautiful Kraków apartment; they seemed to have come through the difficult years unscathed.

However, when the Communist-era files were eventually opened a few years later—against considerable resistance from the Communists themselves—it turned out that the translator had also been an informer. For several decades, starting in the 1950s, he filed monthly written reports to the infamous UB (Office of Public Safety), detailing potentially compromising activities of various people, including members of his wife's cabaret.

This revelation gave new meaning to the word "unbelievable"—except that it was incontrovertibly true. It was the written part of the informing that I found most shocking. It was well known that in the latter days of the Communist era, academics and artists who got permission to travel abroad were required to debrief with the Polish authorities afterward. Most fobbed off the interrogators with trivial information; but writing is an active, deliberate, considered act. And, of course, it leaves a record. How could he?? Apparently, however, the translator was caught in a vise. He wanted to travel—indeed, he needed to travel to remain in touch with English-language literature, and in order to obtain his first passport, during the coldest period of the Cold War era, he had to agree to the terms. After that, he was trapped. Unless he wanted to be outed as a stooge—and to have his passport removed—he had to continue.

Following the revelations, his life was in effect ruined. His wife threw him out of the house (they were then both in their seventies). I wondered, in conversation with her, if, given the circumstances and the trap in which her husband was caught, some understanding was called for; but the realization that the person closest to you has been lying to you systematically for several decades, and delivering information about you to "them," was clearly impossible to live with. The translator moved from Kraków to Warsaw and, after leading the life of a rather insouciant socialite, disappeared from all public life.

This was not murder, torture, or imprisonment, in which the regime specialized in its Stalinist phase, but cooperation with the system's demands continued to exact a steep price—if not in active persecution, then in sacrifice of personal integrity. It was a price that Miłosz understood very well—and which he had refused to pay.

◼ In his late years, Miłosz no longer had to struggle with questions of "the system," as Communist governance came to be called, or his own place within it. But although his active political engagements—so often of an embattled kind—were long over, he remained fully aware of turbulent events elsewhere. He was sufficiently moved by the Yugoslav wars in the 1990s—the only European war since World War II—to write a scorching and unusually direct poetic statement, titled "Sarajevo." Not quite a poem, as he says in his epigraph: "Perhaps this is not a poem, but at least I say what I feel." He does, and what he feels is pure outrage, directed not only at the perpetrators of the war and the Sarajevo massacre, but at all the brave young revolutionaries in other countries who have suddenly gone silent. Above all, his anger is directed at Europe, which stood by as the horrors of the Yugoslav wars un-folded, because, in Miłosz's diagnosis, those who were being murdered were "just barbarians, kill-ing each other."

In other words, the people killed in Sarajevo were—when all was said and done—part of the Other Europe. To him, Europe's indifference in its new iteration suggests that the very idea of "Europe" is a sham; and surely, his outrage was multiplied by his memories of the West's failure to come to Poland's aid during World War II. But even for someone born "after," the failure of the United Nations—and of Europe—to protect the people of Sarajevo was a terrible sign of the democratic world's failure.

▣ Throughout the 1990s, rather amazingly, Miłosz continued to travel internationally, deliver lectures, and engage in live discussions. Then tragedy—this time of a personal kind—struck again. His second wife, so much younger than he was, died of cancer in 2002. Despite the hard-ships of long-distance travel, Miłosz, accompa-nied by his Kraków doctor, made the trip to Berkeley so that he could be with Carol in her last hours. "Orpheus and Eurydice," his poem of mourning for this painful loss, is among his greatest. This is no "ordinary sorrow," as after the

death of his first wife, but rather, a degree of grief
that calls for the universality of myth and its an-
cient, resonant metaphors. The grief is on one
level touchingly personal:

> He remembered her words: "You are a good
>   man."
> He did not quite believe it. Lyric poets
> Usually have—as he knew—cold hearts.
> It is like a condition. Perfection in art
> Is given in exchange for such an affliction.
>
> Only her love warmed him, humanized him.
> When he was with her, he thought
>   differently about himself.
> He could not fail her now, when she was dead.

But as Orpheus descends further underground,
he also travels further into the past:

> Thronging shadows surrounded him.
> He recognized some of the faces.
> He felt the rhythm of his blood.
>
> He felt strongly his life with its guilt
> And he was afraid to meet those to whom
>   he had done harm.

The thronging shadows of the dead, who summon
him even now, have entered his memory and his

very bloodstream—and the guilt, so often present in his writing, is for his own survival. And yet:

> For his defense he had a nine-stringed lyre.
> He carried in it the music of the earth,
>   against the abyss
> That buries all of sound in silence. . . .
> He sang the brightness of mornings and
>   green rivers . . .
> Of colors: cinnabar, carmine, burnt sienna,
>   blue
> Of the delight of swimming in the sea under
>   marble cliffs,
> Of feasting on a terrace above the tumult of
>   a fishing port,
> Of tastes of wine, olive oil, almonds,
>   mustard, salt. . . .
> Of his having composed his words always
>   against death
> And of having made no rhyme in praise of
>   nothingness.

The poem compresses many themes of his late-life poetry—indeed, of his entire oeuvre: regret for his "cold heart," which perhaps allowed him to write through everything and to maintain the detachment enabling much of his vision, but also the redeeming power of poetry, so gloriously evoked here, and his fidelity to the poetry of beauty and meaning rather than of nihilism.

There is also his desire for faith and his inability to embrace it completely:

> Under his faith a doubt sprang up
> And entwined him like cold bindweed.
> Unable to weep, he wept at the loss
> Of the human hope for the resurrection of
> the dead,
> Because he was, now, like every other mortal.
> His lyre was silent, yet he dreamed,
> defenseless.
> He knew he must have faith and he could
> not have faith.

His struggle with religious faith continues, and yet the poem ends on a note of acceptance—of faith, not in the afterlife, but in the here and now, and in the presence, outlasting human life, of nature:

> Sun. And sky. And in the sky white clouds.
> Only now everything cried to him:
> Eurydice!?
> How will I live without you, my consoling
> one!
> But there was a fragrant scent of herbs, the
> low humming of bees,
> And he fell asleep with his cheek on the
> sun-warmed ground.

The meanings of "Orpheus and Eurydice" are multivalent, multiplied by the mythical allusions within the poem's almost epic emotional scale. It is a deeply moving elegy, but one of its interesting aspects is that it is set in the present. In his descent into Hades, the poet finds himself

> . . . walking in a labyrinth,
> Corridors, elevators. The livid light was not
>   light but the dark
> of the earth.
> Electronic dogs passed him noiselessly.
> He descended many floors, a hundred,
>   three hundred, down.

There is poetic exaggeration here, but anyone who has spent time in a big modern hospital will recognize the mood and the description.

The compression of time implicit in "Orpheus and Eurydice," the juxtaposition of classical myth and hypermodernity, can also be read as a summation of Miłosz's thought—or at least one of its important strands. Throughout his work, the governing principles of movement and spatiality take him not only backward, through memory and history, but to the cutting edge of the present. And in his insights into that moment, Miłosz was often prescient and remains surprisingly relevant to our times.

He was highly aware not only of the beauty of nature but of its human despoliations, the pollution of the rivers he loved, the industrial waste-lands, particularly in America. "The thistle, the nettle, the burdock and belladonna / Have a future," he writes in a poem titled "The Thistle, the Nettle"; "Theirs are wastelands / And rusty railroad tracks, the sky, silence." Even when he experiences the return of childhood bliss, as in the essay "Happiness," "the tangible element of flowing time" brings with it a vision not only of a pastoral idyll but of ecological destruction. Before finding his archetypal meadow, he writes, "I went down to my river. It had no lily pads and no calamus, and its reddish color confirmed the presence of chemical plants operated in its upper run. A lonely wild swan kept itself immobile in the middle of oily water, an incongruous sight, suggesting illness or the bird's suicidal intent."

A swan's suicidal intent . . . the pathos of nature in despair. This must have been especially poignant when it touched on landscapes of his childhood. (When I could first return to Poland, after a seventeen-year hiatus, it was the pollution of my childhood rivers—the loss of their purity—that brought home to me, with surprising poignancy, the larger damages we have inflicted on nature.)

In Miłosz's hierarchy of affections, nature was his first and most lasting love. In a moving poem of return, called "Lithuania, After Fifty-Two

Years," the first section is entitled "A Goddess" and begins with a tribute to

> Gaia, first-born daughter of Chaos
> Adorned with grasses and trees, gladdens
>   our eyes
> So that we can agree when naming what is
>   beautiful
> And share with all earthly wanderers our joy.

This does not mean that Miłosz favored a pastoral vision of society, of the kind he critiqued in the hipsters he encountered in California. He loved nature, but he also admired endless human inventiveness and its astonishing innovations, including those enabled by advanced technologies. Still, I think he would have sympathized entirely with today's concerns about climate warming and the increasing sense of alarm about it.

▦ Miłosz's vision was always spacious, reaching imaginatively into the cosmic future as well as into the historical past. And for all his aversion to formal experimentation for its own, usually unintelligible sake, he was willing, even in his late years, to play with new expressive possibilities—as in two surprising recordings, in which love of nature and appreciation of up-to-date technology come together. In the recordings (which can be found on YouTube),

Miłosz reads his own poetry to music composed by his older son, Anthony. Judging by his biographical information, Anthony seems to be as much of a polymath as his father: he studied linguistics, anthropology, and chemistry as well as neurophysiology and neuropharmacology. And, in a generationally fitting addition, he is a composer of electronic music. In one of the YouTube recordings, Miłosz reads, in Polish, his keynote poem "Rivers" to Anthony's spaciously pastoral music. Another recording features Miłosz's moving poem of personal regret, "So Little," to his son's reggae composition. ("I said so little. / Days were short. // Short days. / Short nights. / Short years . . .") It is a wonderfully unexpected but harmonious combination: Miłosz, reading in his soft and clearly articulated Polish, adjusts the rhythms and intonations of his poems to his son's compositions—rendering "Rivers" pensively lyrical and making "So Little" both reflective and almost jazzy. The sense of pleasure in the performance is palpable in the images of father and son, handsomely resembling each other and looking at each other with easy affection. The effect of the recitations would be difficult to replicate in English, but in Polish the musicality of the poems is inflected and increased by the music itself. It is no wonder that Miłosz wrote poems addressed to his native speech. For him, Polish was not only the original language—surely as important as the original river—but the language of internal music, and a crucial thread of internal continuity in a life marked by so many dramatic changes and transformations.

Anthony was an important presence in Miłosz's late years. He wrote a vividly personal preface to Miłosz's *Late Poems* and translated some of them, together with English-speaking colleagues. He also gives us interesting glimpses of his father during his late years. As he testifies, neither Miłosz's age nor his attainment of worldwide fame and critical recognition meant that he rested, even for a moment, on his laurels. Whatever the diversions or the blows of his personal life, he continued to write. Writing, especially writing poetry, was work, but it was also a psychic necessity. He worked systematically and tirelessly, as he had always done, literally almost until his death. In his Kraków apartment, as Anthony tells it, his father got up early each morning and immediately started transcribing (I think the word is accurate here) lines of poetry that occurred to him in the night—perhaps in his dreams, or in that fruitful half-waking state in which ideas can sometimes come to us unbidden and with a strange clarity. "In dreams I saw cities of glass and metal / unceasing fabric of the mind. / Music of the spheres, music of violins and flutes," he wrote in a beautifully suggestive sequence called "Heavenly" in 2003.

Miłosz was opposed to any hint of mystification and, like his fellow exiles, Nabokov and Brodsky, staunchly resistant to psychoanalysis. But two poems about a force he calls his "daimonion" suggest that his poetry emerged from reaches of self that were not entirely under his conscious control. "To My Daimonion," written in the 1990s, is worth quoting at some length:

I

Please, my daimonion, ease off just a bit,
I am still closing accounts and have much
    to tell.
Your rhythmical whispers intimidate
    me. . . .

II

My daimonion, it is certain I could not
    have lived differently.
I would have perished if not for you. . . .
And it seems that while others loved,
Strove, hated, despaired,
I have only been busy with listening intently
To your unclear notes, to change them into
    words.
I had to accept my fate, called today karma,

For it was as it was, though I did not choose it—
And get up every day to honor the work,
Even if there is no guilt of mine in it and no
　　merit.

"Just ease off a bit . . ." The imperative to write could be not only a call to a chosen task but an inwardly propelled tyranny. (Perhaps not only for him: what writer has not sometimes felt at the mercy of the strange compulsion to keep writing, no matter what?) But in a poem written when he was in his nineties, "Without My Daemonion," Miłosz complains that this force hasn't visited him for two weeks—and he feels miserable and mixed up without it:

Daemonion, for two weeks now you've
　　failed to visit me
And I'm becoming the one I'd have always
　　been, without your help.
I look in the mirror and my face finds no
　　favor.
Memory opens up, and it's a horror.

It's unclear just what a daemonion is—but the word derives from the Bible, and it is certainly not a purely rational power. And if, at this late juncture—a few months before his death—Miłosz rued the temporary absence of the mysterious energy driving or enabling him to create poetry, it suggests that writing was as intrinsic to his being as the other vital forces of his body and mind. No matter how self-deprecating he could sometimes be about the very enterprise of poetry ("I am ashamed to write poems"), it was his way of feeling alive—and of taming difficult self-knowledge through the containment of poetic form.

When his sight began to fail him, Miłosz started dictating his morning poems to his secretary and sometimes to his son; his recall of his aural visions was apparently so exact that he included punctuation and line breaks in his dictation. Interestingly, most of his late poems continue the turn to more directly personal expression, even as they revisit the larger themes and questions that drove his work throughout his long life. Aside from his customary self-deprecation, he now allows himself moments of triumph: "And so, after all, I've outlasted you, my enemies!" he writes, although this is quickly followed by a rumination on fate and the dangers of fame. The one undoubted merit for which he is willing to take credit in his old age, as he did before, is his fidelity to the Polish language—which perhaps means fidelity to language altogether, when it serves as the instrument of meaning and expressive beauty.

In a short, late prose note, Miłosz ruefully reflects, "And nothing in me was spontaneous, but under control of the will." Yet perhaps he now felt that he didn't need to protect his self-control or formal discipline quite so much: that the time had come for a more direct, looser kind of disclosure. Even his poems on theological themes contain lighter moments: "Oy, how some Thomas Aquinas or other was needed . . ." Still, the imperatives of memory continue to haunt him, and he now regrets all the stories of people he knew and didn't tell ("I wonder what it was that held me back")—as if that had been a dereliction of duty. At this late stage of life, he is once again poignantly aware that, for many lost lives, he is the only remaining keeper of memory, and that memory is the only stay against death, which in his time had undone so many. He also harkens back to the city of his youth, and its uneasy politics, as in a poem titled "In Vilnius Lilacs Bloom":

At the University, riots of All-Polish Youth,
who demand
that Jewish cadavers, and not only
Christian ones, as heretofore,
be provided for dissections.

The Police lay siege to the dormitory near
Bouffalova Hill and students
douse them from above with water from a
hydrant.

In a poem called "The High-Priest's Son," Miłosz returns to the Jewish theme in a different vein and tries to justify, or at least to explain, the Jewish high priest's rejection of Jesus's divinity. This is an unexpected turn of thought, and I wonder if it had to do, paradoxically, with the pull of conventional Catholicism, which is felt more strongly in Miłosz's late poems. His sympathy for Judaism was never in doubt; but his own, fuller embrace of Catholicism would have made the Jewish rejection of its most fundamental tenet more discomfiting. Indeed, it is perhaps a measure of his sympathy that he now apparently wants to reconcile the two faiths in time to make his own peace with both.

And there is also, to the very end, the urge not only to look back or to admit his all-too-human flaws but the relentless need, which governs so much of his writing, to arrive at an encompassing understanding, both of nature and of the forces governing human existence. He resolutely denied that he was a philosopher, but his temperament and cast of mind were decidedly philosophical—if by that we mean a need to comprehend not only the manifestations of things but the causes and meanings of the phenomena we observe. After a poem called "Heaven," Miłosz adds a prose "Commentary," explaining his complex theology of belief in a divinity—but above all, in human beings.

In "To Nature," he once again makes the distinction between nature, which he loved, and humans, who can feel compassion as well as hatred, who have not only a physical self but a capacity, and the freedom, to make moral choices. These choices are now more simply articulated: "It was in hospitals that I learned humility," he writes in a poem called "Voice." "All evil / Stems from our struggle to dominate our neighbor." There are also, in the last phase of his poetry, moments of capricious humor and lightness as well as quite erotic allusions to women's bodies and forthrightly sexual language about himself.

At the same time, he was of course aware that the inevitable event was approaching—and he confronts it imaginatively in different ways. Sometimes, as in a poem such as "What Do I," he seems to speak from the perspective after death—a state that brings relief from constant concern and imaginative striving, which governed so much of his life:

> . . . What do we care
> that in a great earthquake part of Northern
>   California
> will collapse into the sea,
>
> . . . That the legality of marriage to
>   computers will be debated,

That a planetary cybernetic empire will arise,
What do we care—if in our realm the
    world's din is fading
And we enter Another, beyond time and
    space.

Elsewhere, as in a poem titled "Heavenly," Miłosz imagines himself quite soberly, and without special sorrow, within the land of the dead, which, in tandem with William Blake, he envisions as a more intense version of the here and now; a realm of "eternal intellectual hunts / a chase after ever self-renewing meaning." His paradise, even at this late date, was not a place of rest but of effort and continuing quests; this is of course a hopeful vision—not of death, really, but of eternal life.

Above all, in his late poems Miłosz once again reaches back, with renewed astonishment, to his own beginnings and to Lithuania, with all its local names and landscapes. "I hail from another dimension in which I lived / At the start of an elapsed century far from cities," he writes in an untitled verse. These too are poems of distances and the great spans he traveled in time and history, in geography and symbolic space. Separation and its losses were both a cause of pain and the exilic advantage: the sources both of his restless questioning, in which nothing could be taken for granted, and of his spacious, far-reaching vision, in which anything could be imagined.

Miłosz's final years were blessedly free of external turmoil, and his last poems are a testament to a new kind of freedom. Here's his penultimate poem, "On Salvation":

Saved from possessions and honors,
Saved from bliss and from worry,
Saved from life and enduring,
Saved.

He was clearly ready to face death, and his very last poem, entitled "Goodness," offers a tender picture of Oscar de Lubicz Milosz, his distant relative and mystical poet whom he met during his first, youthful visit to Paris, and who introduced him to the writings of Swedenborg and Simone Weil. Miłosz revered Oscar throughout his life, without always being able to follow in his footsteps. Speaking of his predecessor's arcane theology in the poem, he says that "this was already something my mind could not grasp." Miłosz couldn't have known that this would be his final note—the note of perplexity and wonder, which sent him, to the end, on his relentless quests for further, deeper, more complete understanding.

Miłosz died in 2004 at his home in Kraków. His funeral in that city was a majestic affair, of the kind more familiar in the nineteenth century—the funerals of Victor Hugo, for example, or of Frédéric Chopin. Great crowds lined the streets, and dignitaries attended. After a service at the beautiful Mariacki Church, built in the fourteenth century in the Rynek, Miłosz was moved to the Skalka Roman Catholic Church—a kind of equivalent of Westminster Cathedral in London. In front of the church, Seamus Heaney, Robert Hass (Miłosz's main translator), and Adam Zagajewski, a friend and undoubtedly his poetic successor in the next generation, read Miłosz's beautiful tribute to his birthplace, "In Szetejnie," in all the languages Miłosz had mastered: Polish, French, English, Russian, Lithuanian, and Hebrew. (Sadly, Zagajewski died even as I was writing this, at the age of seventy-five.)

During his long lifetime, Miłosz, like his first fictional hero, mentioned in his Nobel speech, traveled over great distances, in every sense of the word, but in the end, he came back almost full circle to a city not far from his origins, to rest, surely, in peace. Not immediately, however: in a final irony, even while the funeral was going on, new battles, of the kind with which we have since become all too familiar, were brewing, as protesters tried to disrupt the proceedings on the grounds that Miłosz was anti-Polish and anti-Catholic, and had apparently signed a petition supporting "gay and lesbian freedom of speech and assembly." Luckily, Miłosz was not only guiltless of the nonsensical charges, but had very good connections in the upper echelons of the Catholic church, and Pope John Paul II, along with Miłosz's personal confessor, issued a public statement to certify that the poet had received the last sacraments. This put a stop to the absurdist protests, but these were, especially in Poland, a portent of things to come.

Politics, in its new guise, didn't leave Miłosz alone even after his death, and I wonder what he would think about the next turn of the historical wheel, evident not only in Poland but in so many parts of the world that have witnessed new forms of ideological conflict and a worrying decline of democracy. He probably would have answered that "turn of the wheel" was the wrong metaphor or that, in relation to history, all metaphors are lacking. History doesn't repeat itself exactly, nor does it necessarily swing like a pendulum. And it certainly doesn't progress straight as an arrow.

We don't have this most thoughtful of men to help us work through such questions anymore. Miłosz's work, however, remains as pertinent as ever. The relevance of *The Captive Mind*, in particular, continues unabated, and references to it crop up regularly in critiques of today's "group-think." The demands of contemporary identity politics are hardly as onerous as the imperatives of dialectical materialism in its Soviet guise, but the pressures of political correctness, coming from the right and the left sides of the political spectrum, can exercise their own tyranny. The punishments meted out by "cancel culture" are certainly not as brutal as being imprisoned or having one's passport revoked for incorrect views—but they have real consequences for their recipients, ranging from unpleasant forms of ostracism to people losing their jobs or having their books revoked by various cultural gatekeepers or editors who, with considerable pusillanimity, buckle to collective pressure. Some supposedly retrograde authors are "canceled" altogether: a form of moral righteousness with very unpleasant historical connotations.

It is hard to know whether these are phenomena of the moment or deeper and more lasting trends—but navigating the mazes and pressures of contemporary life takes considerable strong-mindedness. It requires the ability to distinguish between fake and real news, between ideas borrowed from our peers and our own convictions. And, as Miłosz already saw among the California hipsters no less than in the conformist middle classes, such resilience is not cultivated in contemporary democracies. For the younger generations especially, distinguishing groupthink from individual thought is made vastly more difficult by the reach of that omnipresent, political and personal, Janus-faced demiurge of digital technologies. Here, too, Miłosz foresaw what was coming, and as his imaginative travels took him into the far-flung future as well as the historical past, his poems allude to the ubiquity and tyranny of the internet and the coming "cybernetic empire."

The Captive Mind is a book that still, quite urgently, matters—and so does Miłosz's insistence on the value of memory. In his poetry, memory is most often poignantly personal and particular, but in his Nobel lecture, he worried about the possibility of wider, historical amnesia. He mentioned a large number of books propounding the idea that the Holocaust never happened; since then, this abhorrent form of historical denial has only gained adherents, especially among the young. In this respect, Miłosz thought (perhaps too wishfully) that the Other Europe and Poland, in particular, had some advantages over the ostensibly more advanced West. In his Nobel lecture, he cites the names of two friends who perished in the Katyn massacre—the wholesale murder of over 20,000 Polish officers by the Soviet Union during World War II—an event still officially denied by the Soviet authorities when Miłosz was writing but which was the subject of collective rage. Indeed, the denial undoubtedly stoked the rage. But Miłosz's point was also that it is through particular memories—the names of his two friends, for example—that we gain a felt understanding of larger history.

In today's Poland—and perhaps all of eastern Europe as well—the memory of twentieth-century cataclysms continues to be vividly alive, even among the younger generations. This is not only a question of education, which, Miłosz thought, was in this respect so sadly lacking in America and elsewhere. Poland, after all, was, between 1939 and 1945, the center of the inferno—and almost everyone who lived through it suffered losses, of family members, of communities, of friends. Moreover, the postwar decades, all the way until 1989, were a period of memory suppression and denial. The period after the emergence of the suppressed memories—of the Holocaust, of the non-Communist resistance, of communism itself—from the historical freezer witnessed an almost palpable return of the past, with all its personal and collective losses, and all its political passions. The much-vaunted end of history was, in Poland, a period of history's return.

But the return of collective memory didn't save nations from the next wave of reaction. After the heady liberal interregnum, both Poland and Hungary have adopted what the Hungarian government quite openly terms "illiberal democracy." The attempts to control interpretations of history through government diktats have been a salient part of this profoundly antidemocratic trend. I wonder what Miłosz would have made of such developments; I wonder if he would have heard clear echoes of prewar authoritarianism or if he might have seen it as another phase of the nationalist trend he so opposed, which was interrupted by the war and by the forced adoption of communism. Or perhaps he might have agreed with analysts who think that the contemporary liberal ethos, complete with its identity politics, was imposed on eastern Europe forcibly and too fast by the western parts of it—the parts that still stand for the norm, and for Europe itself.

I very much wish I could conduct a follow-up interview with Miłosz to find out what he might think of such developments. His opinions were more trustworthy than most; there was no one less prone to ideological distortion or to political positions uninformed by reality. And there was no one—certainly, no writer I can think of—with greater, or more consciously observed, historical experience.

As for the great body of his poetry, it is studied and read in many parts of the world, and its importance surely won't wane as long as poetry continues to matter. I think it would have been a special satisfaction to him to see the allusions to his work made by Iranian or Chinese literati whom I met at various conferences in the years after his death, and for whom twentieth-century Polish poetry had a special importance. It was, after all, a poetry of resistance.

We no longer have Miłosz with us, but we have his enormous legacy to draw on, with its challenge to truthfulness and three-dimensional thought, the meaningful beauty of his poetry, and its grounded, time- and space-spanning vision. Beginning in an obscure corner of the Other Europe, he gave us the world.

WORKS CITED

All quotations by Czesław Miłosz come from the following volumes:

The Captive Mind, translated by Jane Zielonko. New York: Vintage Books, 1981. Copyright © by Czeslaw Milosz, used by permission of The Wylie Agency LLC.

Facing the River, translated by Czesław Miłosz and Robert Haas. New York: Ecco Press, 1995.

Native Realm: A Search for Self-Definition, translated by Catherine S. Leach. Garden City, NY: Doubleday, 1968.

New and Collected Poems: 1931–2001, translated by Czesław Miłosz and Robert Haas. New York: Ecco Press, 2001. Excerpts from "Encounter," "Ballad of Levallois," "Faith," "Hope," "A Poor Christian Looks at the Ghetto," "Café," "In Warsaw," "Dedication," "Child of Europe," "You Who Wronged," "What Once Was Great," "A Treatise on Poetry," "Ode to a Bird," "My Faithful Mother Tongue," "To Raja Rao," "The Year," "Elegy for N.N.," "Six Lectures in Verse," "Gift," "From the Rising of the Sun," "The Separate Notebooks," "A Portal," "After Paradise," "Caffé Greco," "A Confession On Parting with My Wife, Janina," "And Yet the Books," "In Common," "Conversations with Jeanne,"

"Translating Anna Swir on an Island of the Caribbean,"
"City of My Youth," "The Thistle the Nettle," "Lithuania
After Fifty-Two Years," "So Little," "Heavenly." Copyright © by The Czeslaw Milosz Estate. Used by permission of Harper Collins Publishers.

Selected and Last Poems, 1931–2004, translated by Czesław
Miłosz and Robert Haas. New York: Ecco Press, 2011.
Excerpts from "Classmate," "Orpheus and Eurydice,"
"To My Daimonion," "Without My Daimonion," "In
Vilnius Lilacs Bloom," "Voice," "What Do I Care,"
"Heavenly," "Untitled," "On Salvation." Copyright ©
1988, 1991, 1995, 2001, 2004, 2006 by The Czesław Miłosz
Estate. Used by permission of Harper Collins Publishers.

A Treatise on Poetry, translated by Czesław Miłosz and Robert Haas. New York: Ecco Press, 2001.

Visions from San Francisco Bay, translated by Richard Lou-
rie. New York: Farrar, Straus & Giroux, 1982. Copyright
© by Czeslaw Milosz, used by permission of The Wylie
Agency LLC.